Acknowledgements.


First & foremost I would like to thank my Mum, thanks for helping me with this book, you have always been there & you are my biggest supporter in so many ways, you inspire me, I love you Mum!!

I would also like to thank my publishers at Aloe Jimmy Publishing for making this book possible, thank you Jimmy & James for being part of this with me, thank you for your friendship, I look forward to working more with both of you!

I would like to thank all the people I have met & worked with along my business journey who have helped to inspire & educate me in the world of entrepreneurs & business, as well as everyone who has given me a chance to bring my business that much further, with my thanks to everyone who has helped with the launch venue for this book. David Vane & SBGN, Nicky Curtis & Solent Creatives, Wildern School & everyone at the D.@rt Centre, Andrew Skinner & Arts & Heritage Southampton & venues, The Boutique Village, Harbour Lights Cinema, ISTC Cricket Camp & Southern entrepreneurs.

I would also like to say thanks to all who have inspired me, through my favourite horror films, music & gothic inspiration which has been a huge part of my lifestyle through gothic culture for many years & has now given birth to this gorgeous little book which I am so proud of creating through allowing my mind to run wild with velvet gothic hues.

Anyone who I have forgotten please accept my apologies, I really do appreciate everyone who has helped along the way.

.

Emma Morrissey

United Kingdom

Website: www.emzportraitscrafts.wordpress.com

First published in Great Britain by Aloe Jimmy Publishing in 2015

ISBN: 978-0-9926276-5-2

British Library Cataloguing-in-publication Data

A catalogue record for this book is available from the British Library

Published by Aloe Jimmy Publishing 2015.

# Gothic Poetry

## A collection from the crypt.

Written & Illustrated by Emma Morrissey BA.

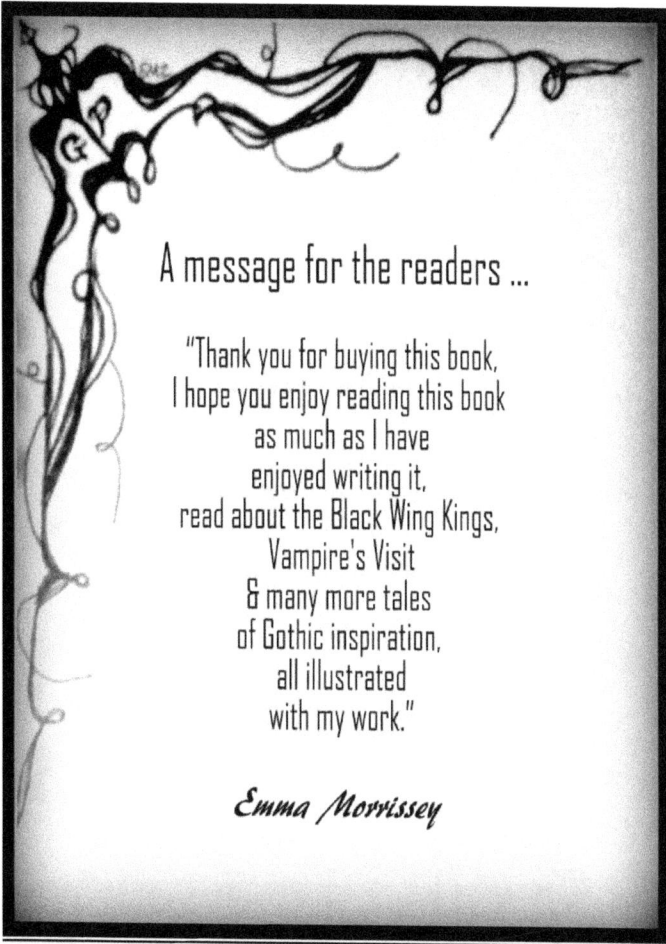

# A message for the readers ...

"Thank you for buying this book,
I hope you enjoy reading this book
as much as I have
enjoyed writing it,
read about the Black Wing Kings,
Vampire's Visit
& many more tales
of Gothic inspiration,
all illustrated
with my work."

*Emma Morrissey*

# -Gothic Poetry -

## A Collection from the crypt.

Black Rose Illustration, pastel on black paper.

# Tales from the quill.

Tales from the quill,

As ink makes its mark.

Elegant glides speaking of mysteries in the dark.

Legends & fables told in rhyming form,

Reminding all of stories, far from the norm.

Tales of wolves & sharpened teeth,

Long cloaks with deadly secrets lurk beneath.

All these stories written in hand,

Filling our imagination with a darker land.

Men & woman,

Writing tales of mystery,

I wonder,

Do you have a story?

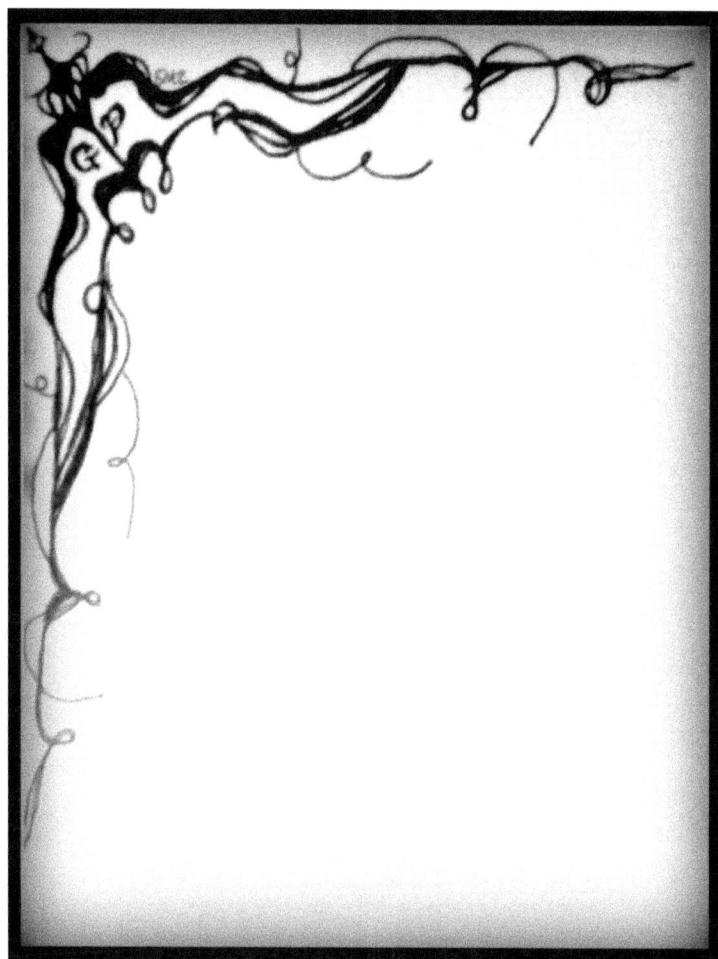

# *Stars*

Stars sparkling on a crisp clear night,

A chill twirling its magic as its icicles bite.

Clear sky like a velvet cloak,

Sparling spots of light settled as the vamps come out to gloat.

A full moon tonight,

A wonder to behold,

In awe are furry creatures,

And the fanged ones untold.

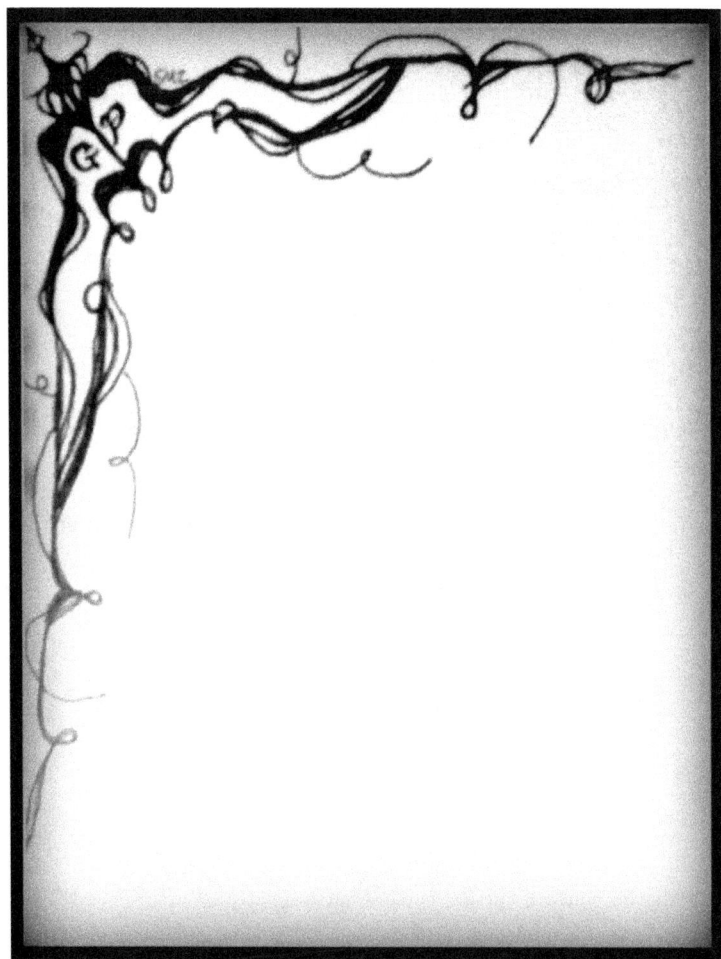

# Woman

Woman of black attire with an elegant awe,

Many dark mistresses have taken this style & more.

Charcoal hair with the palest skin,

Many an hour spent to achieve such pure porcelain.

Eyes encased with black & sometimes the deepest green hues,

To magnify their stares as they look straight through you.

Many appear but not many are seen,

Oh yes,

Many mystery of a gothic lady remain unforeseen.

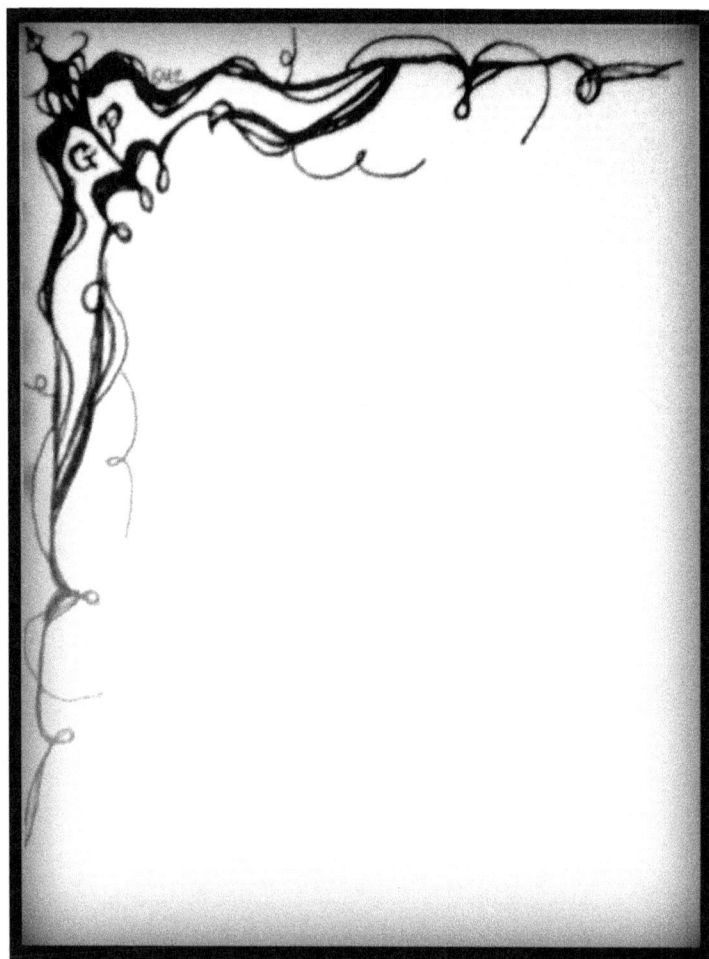

# Fury of the Beast.

Fury of the beast with its teeth rearing at its prey,

Oh what morsel will my hunger feast on today?

Horns sharp & nostrils flair,

Why don't they run?

Are they transfixed by my stare?

Making its move as it bends it back leg,

Awaiting the attack,

To jump at its prey to their dread.

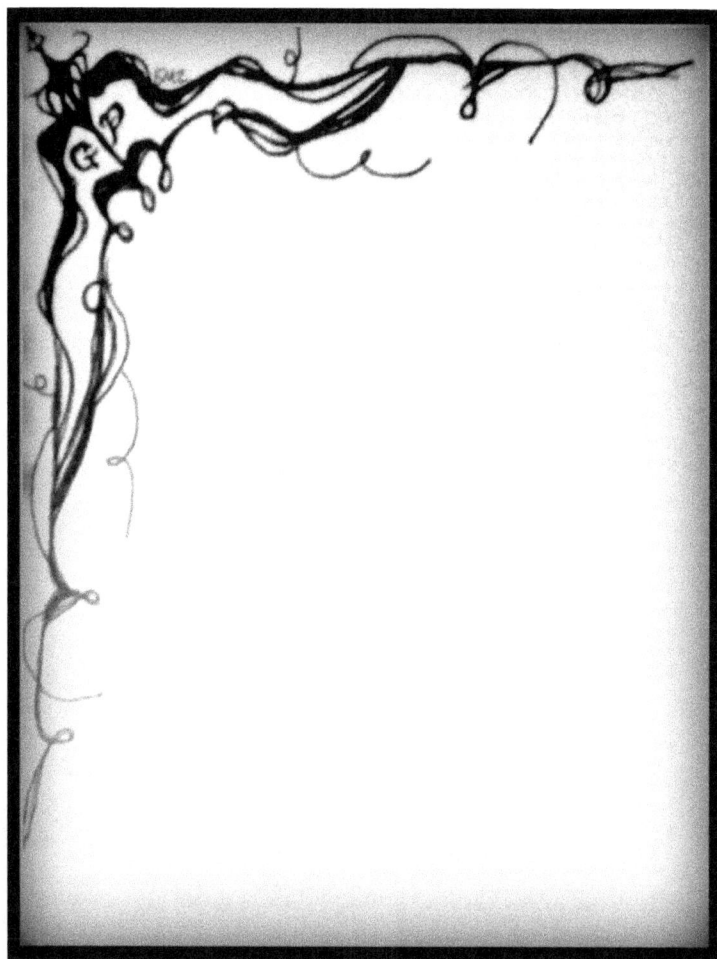

# Dark Knight.

Dark light

Dark knight

Always covers the sky,

Dark light

Dark knight

Floating past my eye,

Dark light

Dark knight

Beautiful deadly wings

Dark light

Dark knight

Darkness of the kings

# The Redditch Riddlier storyteller.

The Redditch riddlier story teller,

Oh fancy fairy of old glen diary

Gave such dance on kitchen light,

But who of times two did fancy dance to?

Divide that by golden moonlight.

Redditch riddlier skipped through great Kidderminster,

Collecting more riddles for fun,

His friends the mice hadn't seen riddle but thrice,

So left for buns on toasted rice.

Poor riddlier,

Tired from his riddles of fun,

'I wonder if I should skip under the sun'.

So riddlier did just that,

Rested upon his tall, tophat,

Sleeping under sun rays watched by neighbour's fat cat.

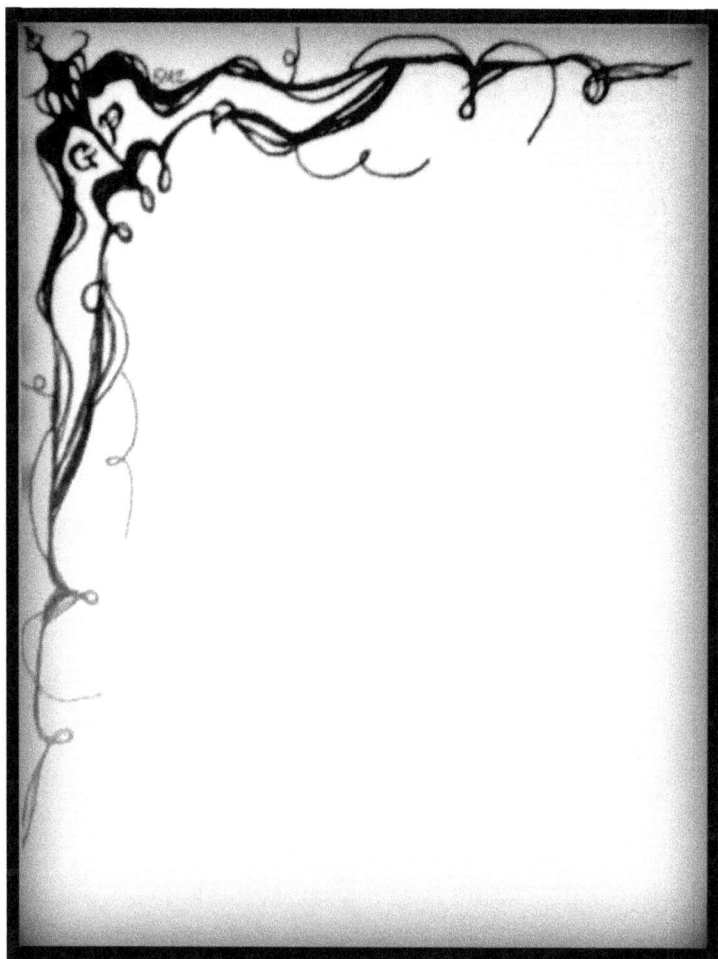

## Magic Jacket.

Magic Jacket,

All seams & pockets,

Fitted & buttoned in black suede. Lining of red,

Collar fastened velvet thread,

For me, beautifully made.

Gothic jacket makes the scene,

The count of vamp-ish dreams,

Pockets of silk,

Frills a slight tilt,

Gothic jacket of my dreams.

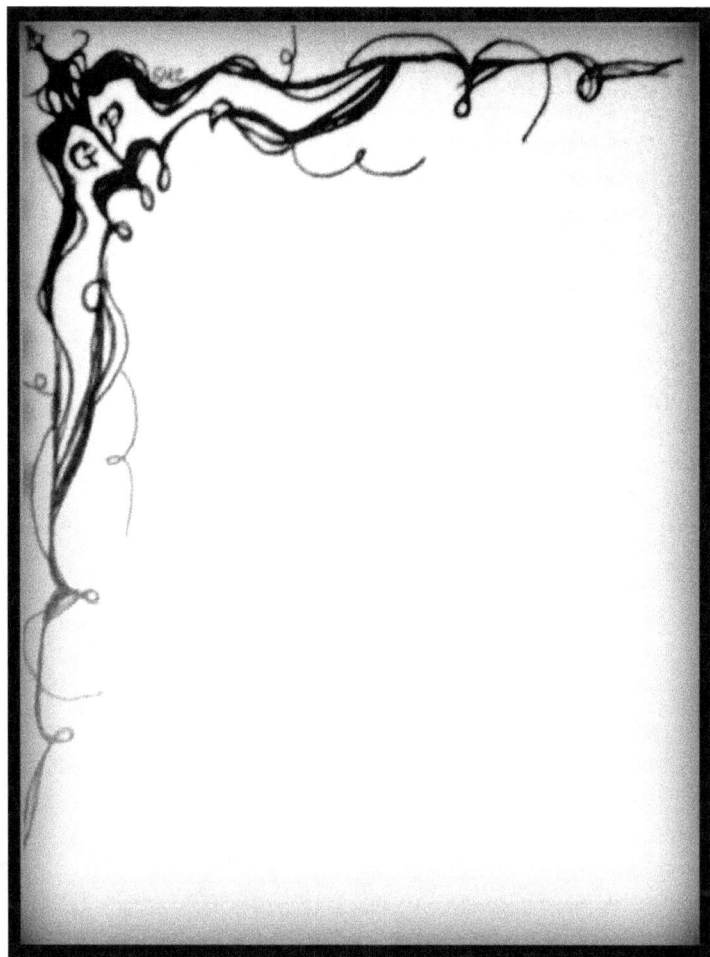

# Great Old Oak

The great old oak was of mystery to us local folk,

As it leaves never moved in the wind.

Like a dark shadow at night,

It cast looming fright as passers-by felt its icy sting.

Old oak tree stood amongst the forestry,

Animals kept their distance;

For tales of this old oak from many spooked folk, loomed an eerie silence.

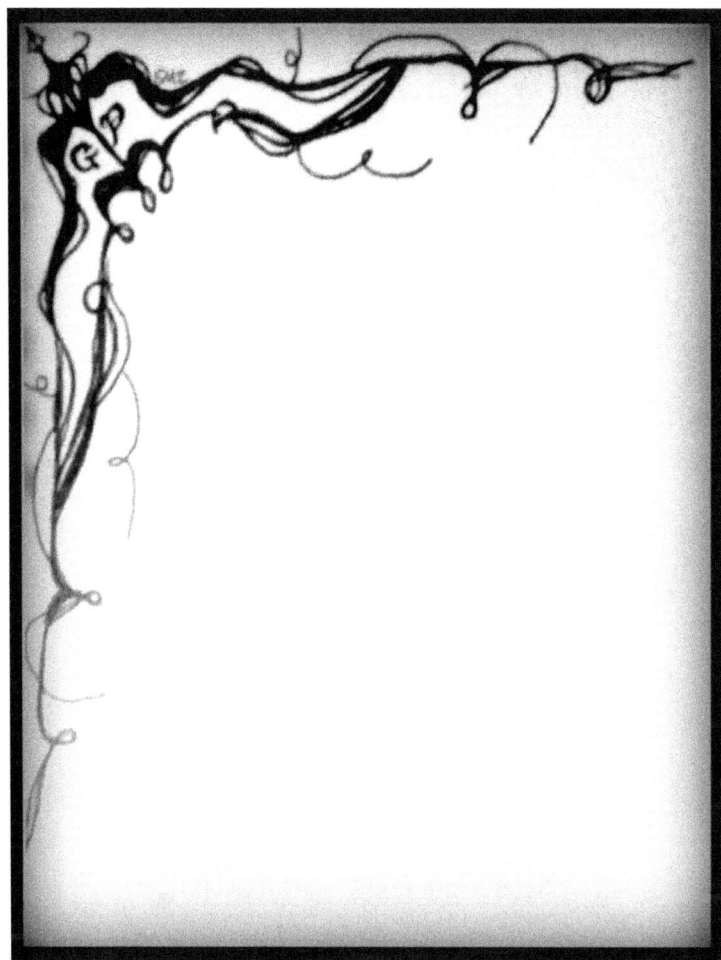

# The Black Wing Kings.

The Black wing kings,

The dark wing kings

Watch over us all as we dream in fright,

Dark wing kings,

Of the black wing kings

Will see us through the night.

The Black wing kings

See all our frightening's, as we fuel their life,

Oh black winged things

Of the night time king,

Feed on our sleep's strife.

The holey souls of those black winged things

Sample our fright as their power,

The dark wing kings,

The black wing kings

See us through the nightmares of the midnight hour.

Cells, acrylic on canvas

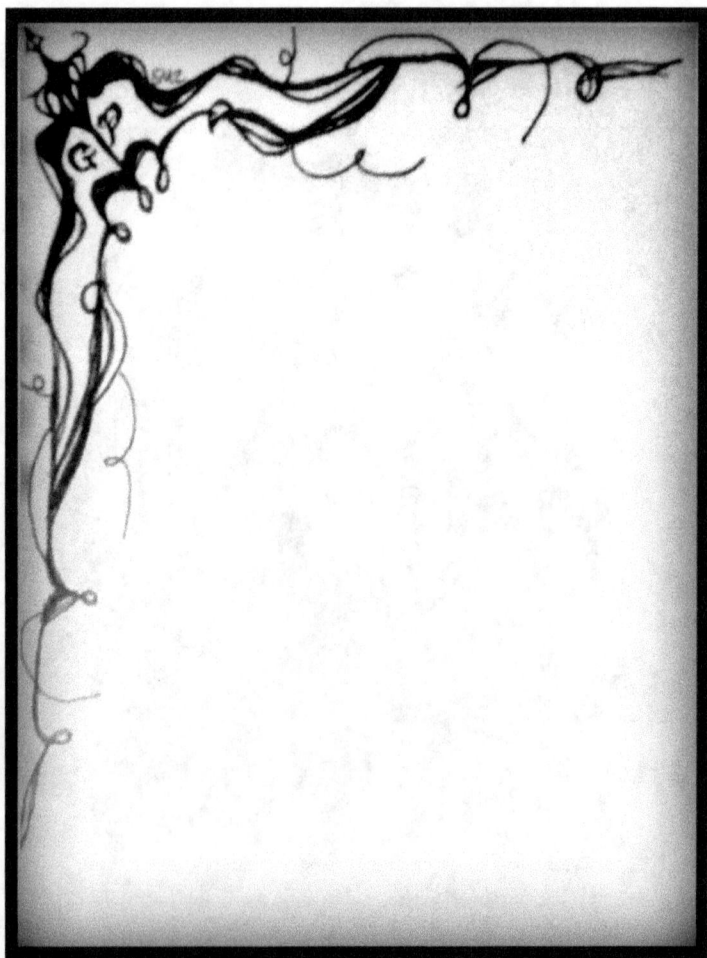

# The Fairies Broken Wing.

Every day at fifteen to may

The fairy nursed her wing,

Each moon long after noon

The fairy bathed in milk.

Her broken wing,

She would sing as she clocked in purple silk,

The fairy queen of another dream

Had met with fairies wing.

Offering fairy rice to soak up the broken slice

As fairy bathed again not in pain.

Rising from the milky suds,

Fairy glowed inside from new buds

Fairies wing had grown again.

Tophat Goggle Rat Illustration, ink on paper

# Tophat Goggle Rat.

Tophat goggle rats,

The sleepy slows & the rascal cats.

Dark of the night & close of the crow,

Adorn rat's tophat & goggles you know.

Stay on top said Mr Flop,

As rat straightened his tale,

Goggles up high for a rat of so high,

Never quite had up for bale.

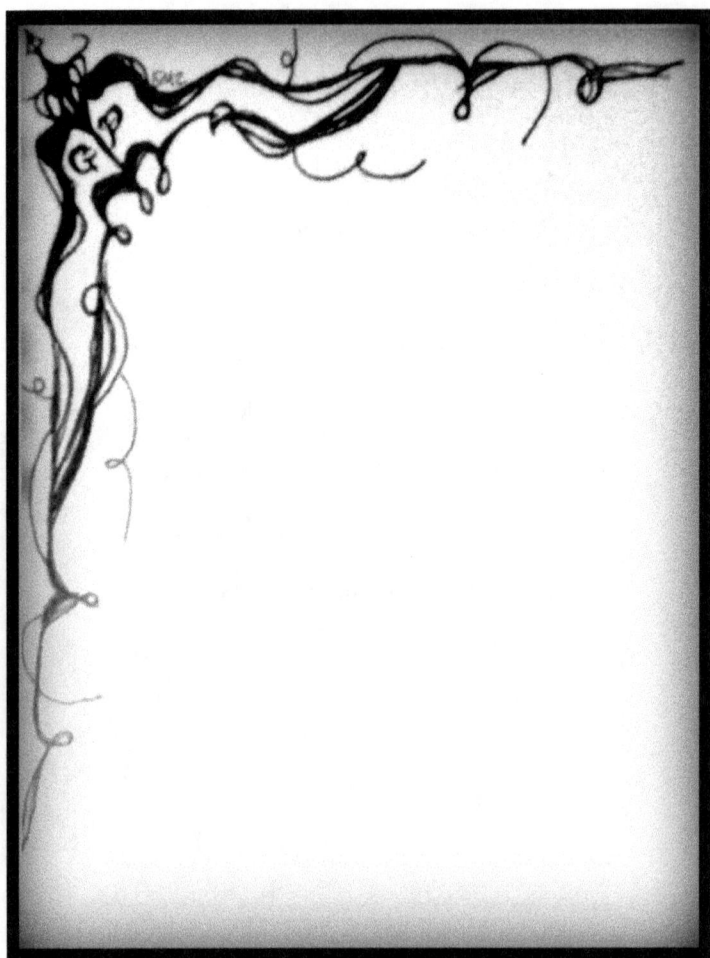

# Mr Potts.

Mr Potts counting knots,

Glancing at the howling sky.

Taking Martha aside down her pride, as she cleans the table high.

Glistening bubbles from sulking suds troubles,

Mopping up days dirty heads,

Martha stops short,

Her breath sudden caught, as Mr Potts steams ahead.

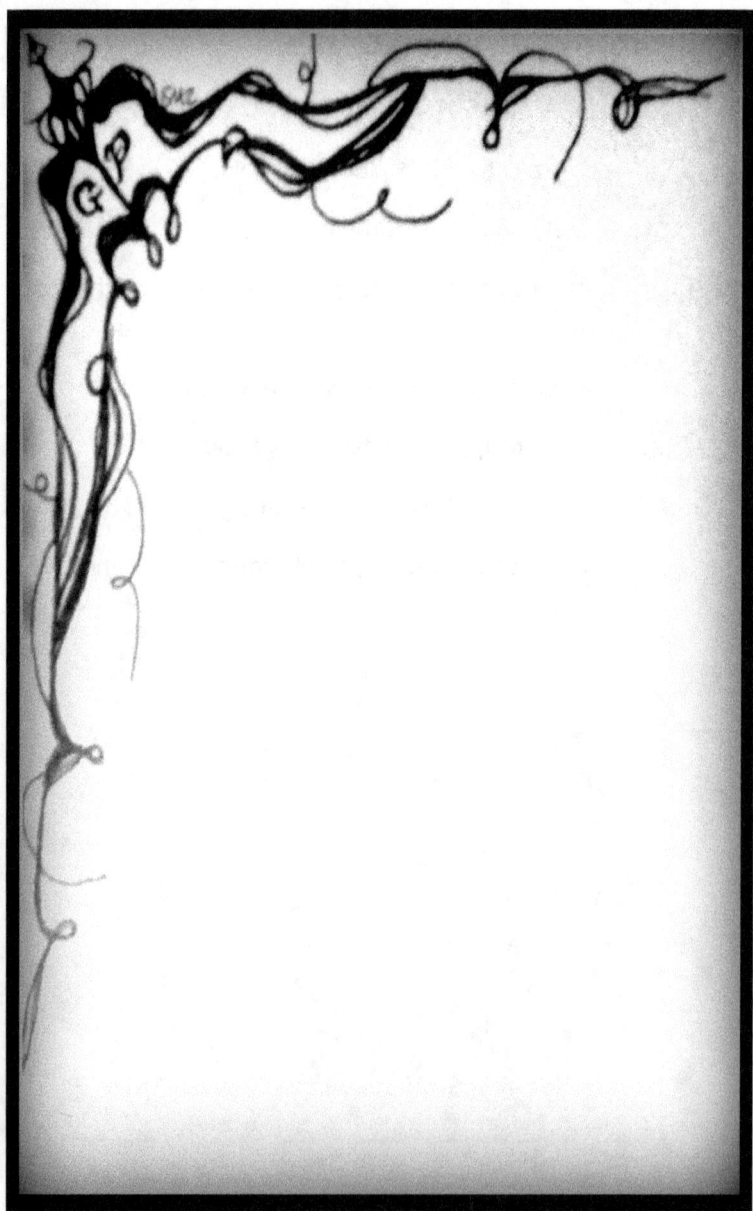

# Snowy Step from the Owl Lep.

Snowy step form the owl lep,

As wind howls into the night sky it crept.

Snowy skies from darkened heights,

As Mr Potts plays piano in the pale moonlight,

Playing keys on bended knees to the moths in the night.

Snowy steps from the owl crept,

Take with me Mr Potts moths through the night as they dance,

Dance to every step.

# Midnight Bites.

They lurk in the dirt

Travelling from night to night.

Bites, frights & all that feeds,

One bite from those mites are all they need.

Bites you don't feel,

They make you think they're not real,

But only we know what's truly at stake.

For staying awake is a dreadful state,

For the awful marks they make.

Make sure when you sleep,

Only holiness you keep

So bites will cease to find your neck.

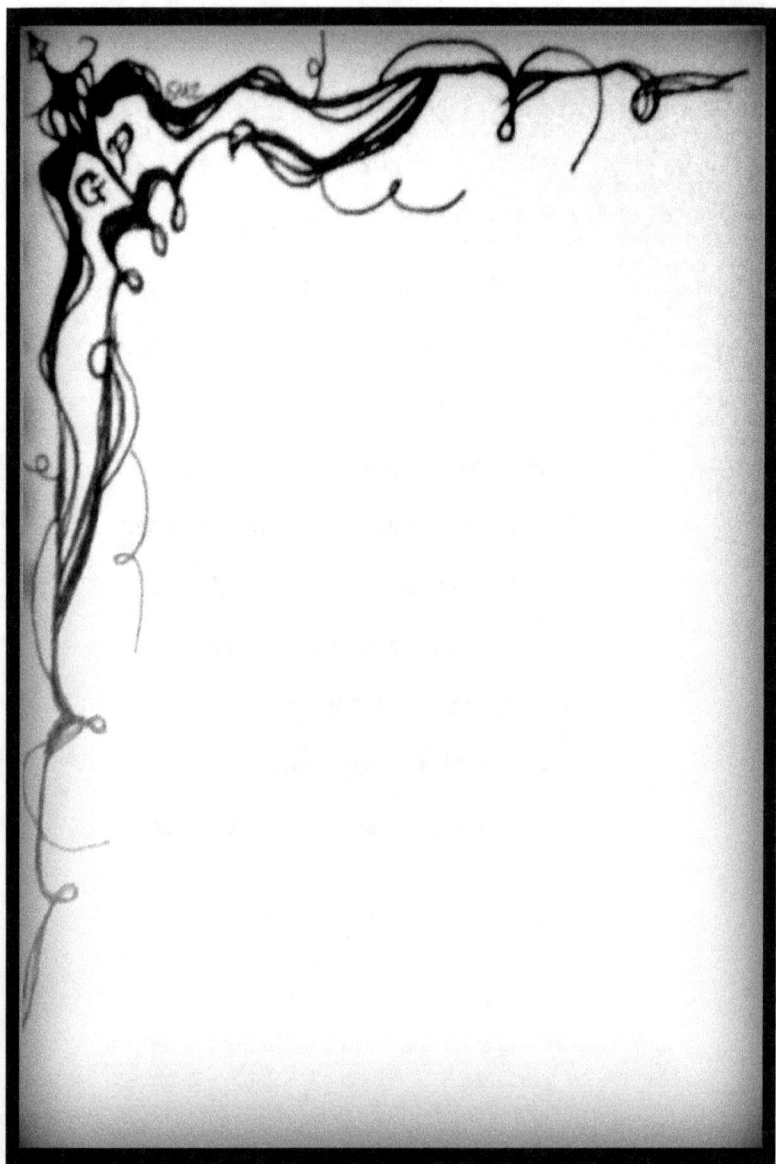

# *Howling.*

Howl,

Now,

Forever at the full moon.

Howling,

Prowling,

They return themselves at noon.

Find them,

Hide them,

They hunt the cold evenings in the night.

Howling,

Howling.

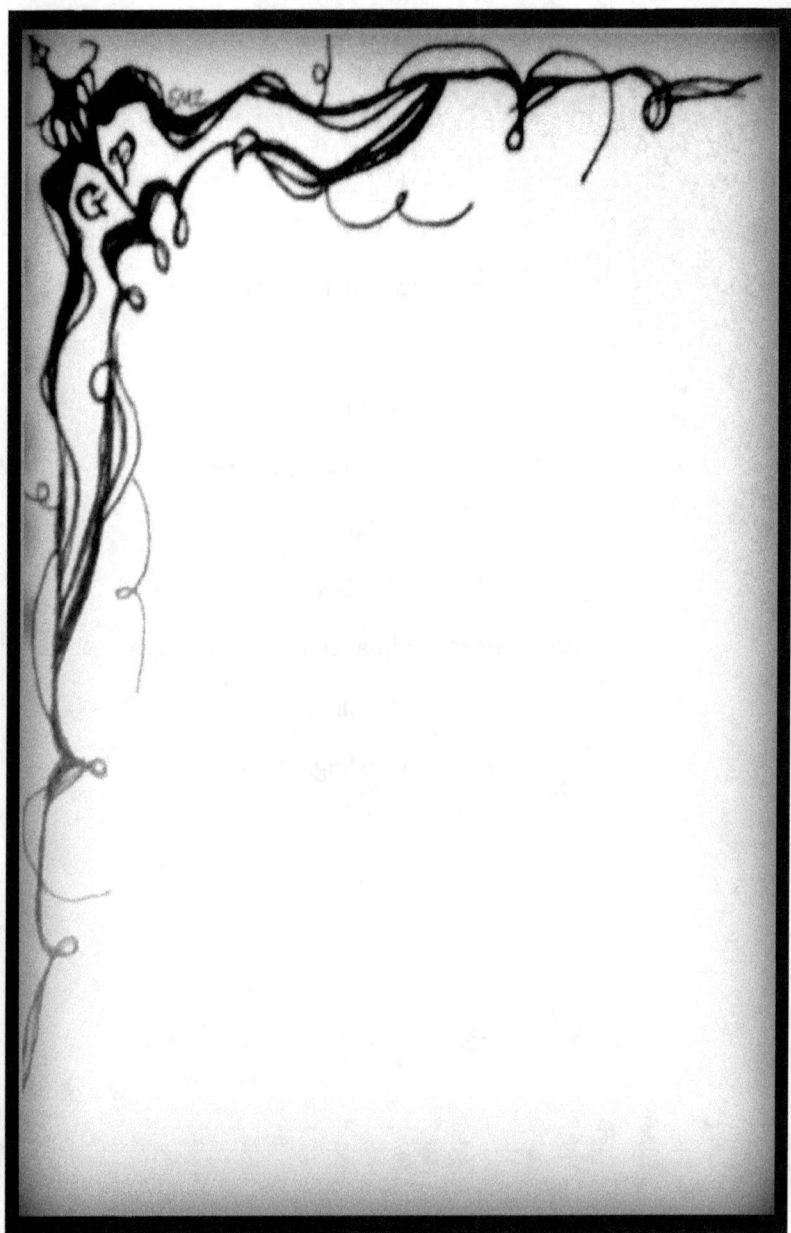

# Black is the colour.

Black with Red,

Black with green,

Black with purple,

Black with blue,

All richly dark will see me through.

Black with Victorian vibe,

Black with Lolita dainty,

All these gothic hues fill me plenty.

Black with buckles,

Black with lace,

Black with ruffles are never out of place.

Black is the colour,

Black is the heart,

The heart of the gothic King & Queen,

The Gothic revolution starts.

# Nameless Gnomes.

Nameless gnomes from sicken grove, they watch the vamps at night.

Those clever gnomes sat pleasant at home, from their window ledge saw a terrible fright.

The vamps brought back a maiden it seemed that, as she laid flat on vamps back, "What a shameful sight", said gnome to his wife,

As they prayed for maiden's ghost to attack.

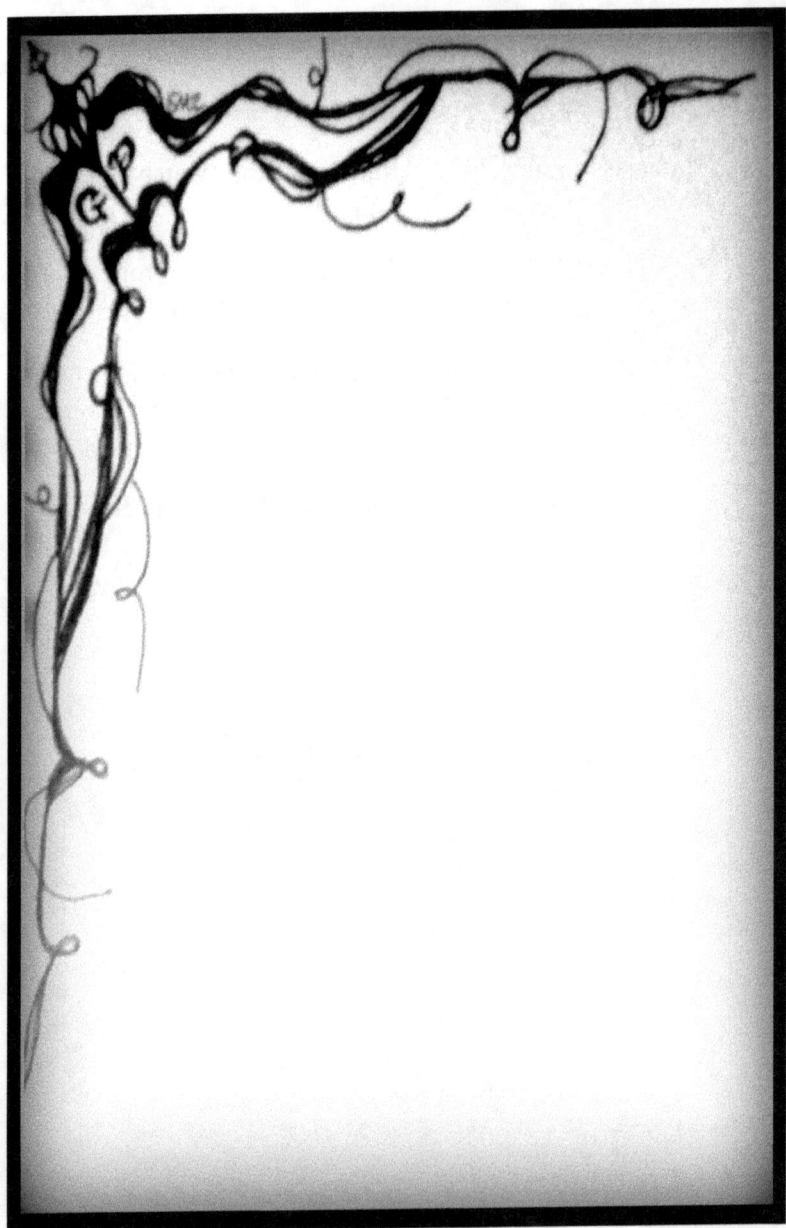

## Pots & Pans Mother Ann.

Pots & pans Mother Ann said Martha,

Oh how you grind so well,

For all in store as she polished the floor,

His mark down Mother Stairwell.

Oh & you bark Mother Ark, showing your wings as you fly,

But those poor pots & pans Mother Ann,

Never cease as they linger to dry.

Missypot Skeleton Illustration from my 'Steampunk
Collection' ink on paper

# Fat Cat.

A fur cape of black said fat cat,

"Oh you do wear it well, if only Mouse Gertrude could fathom the attitude but her taste is not swell".

"What a ghastly hat!"

Said old cat Pat,

As it stared at her all bony & clawed.

"Fear not moggy sort, it is not but

Skeletal caught, it sits proud above my head, what a sort!"

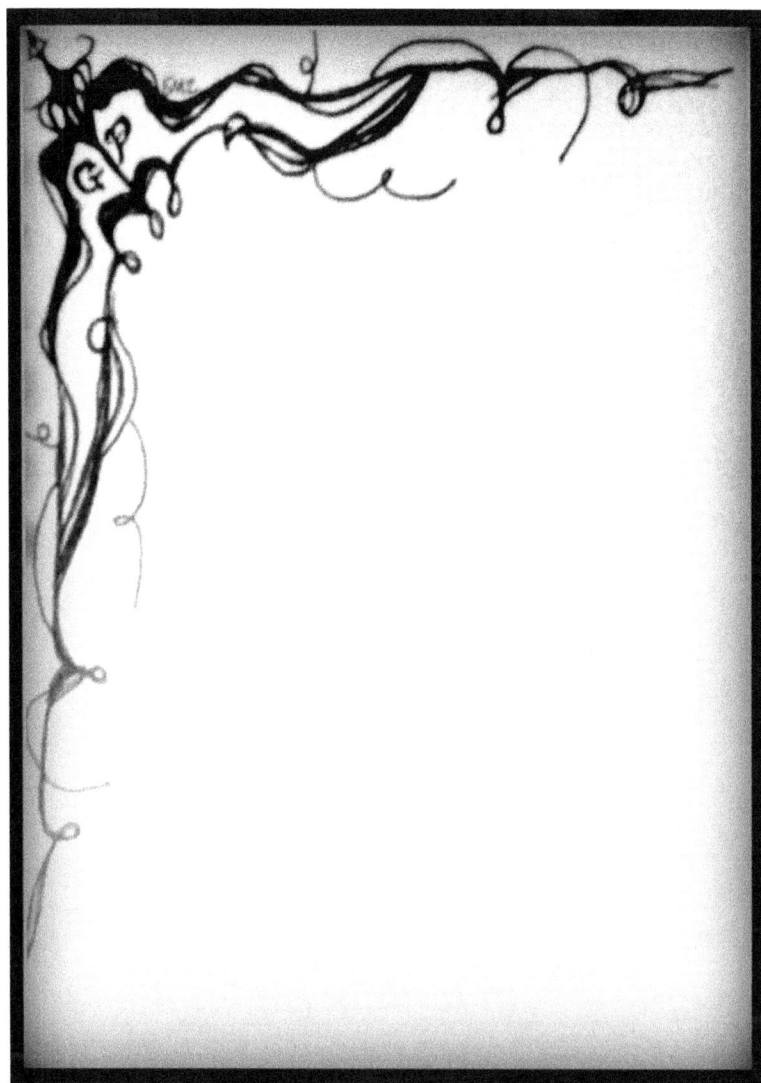

# Nixy Knock the ticking clock

"Nixy Knock",

Said the ticking clock,

Ticks & tocks to the beat as it locks.

Hands of time as the clock strikes nine,

Always the same as before said chime.

Friends with every watch that sings,

The click each notch as their time comes to ring.

"Nixy knock",

Said the ticking clock, always keeps me on time.

Nixy knock the ticking clock Illustration, ink on paper

## Goblin Glares.

Goblin glares,

A thing of nightmares,

As they sprint around the tree trunks & stare.

All the same size & ugly eyes,

As they swarm local folk with terror.

Locals hide from them as goblins run to them, always chanting their song.

These goblins of the forest,

Never knowingly honest, winter terrors have begun.

# Pale as the pink Rose.

Pale as the pink rose,

Makeup ghostly & pure,

Pale against black overtones

Is less really more?

Red is my crown,

Pale pink linen skin,

Black is my overtone,

But colourful beauty within.

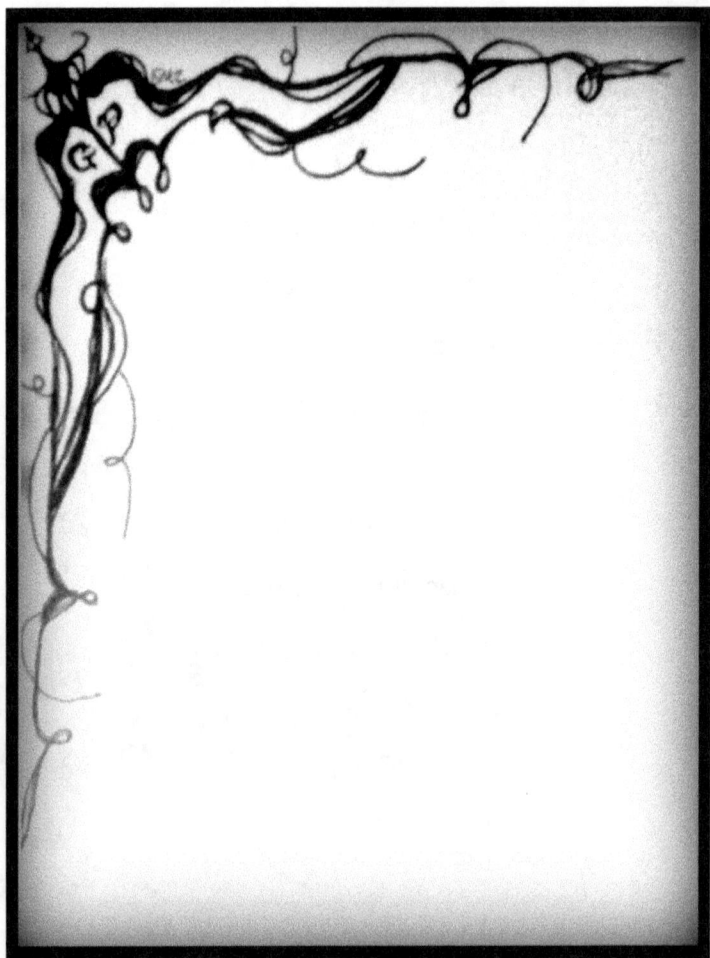

# The Black Rose.

Petals of charcoal,

Stem of iron,

Petals soft to touch,

Black as the gargoyle.

Only one place to find such a dark beauty,

Roses of rich reds,

For the Gothic Beauty.

Black Rose,

Alone in the field,

Tempted to sway in the wind,

Picked by the knight,

For his beauty's delight

As she craves what usual roses can't bring.

Junior Skeleton Illustration from my 'Steampunk Collection'
ink on paper

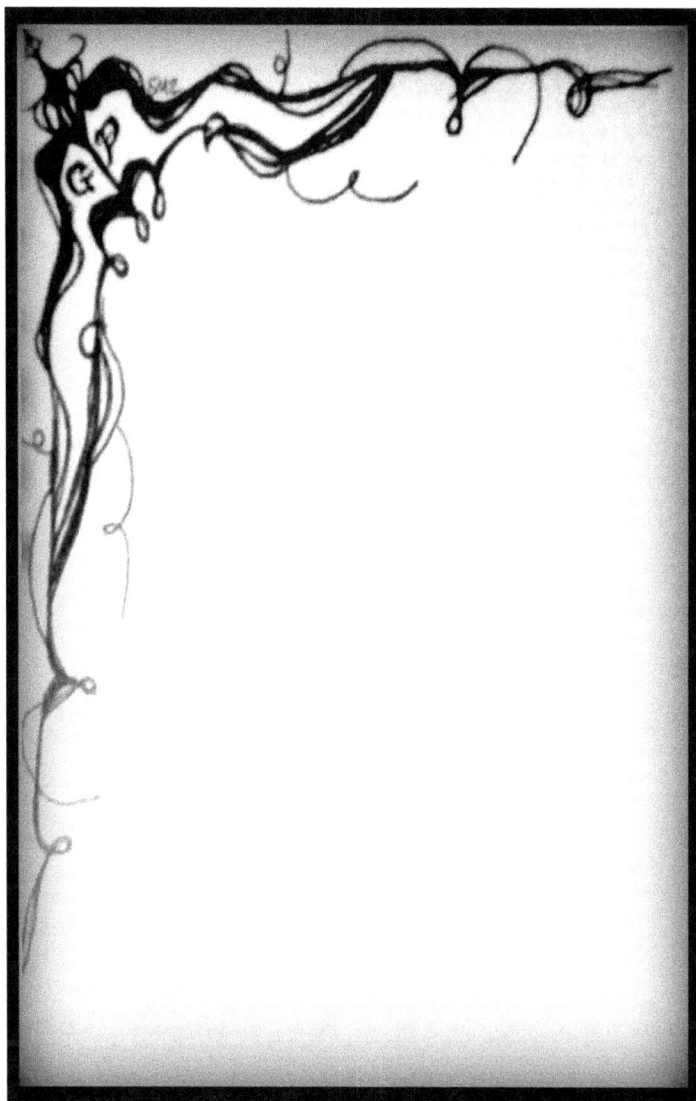

# The Crypt.

A darkening crypt of souls rested.

Cooling in the night breeze,

These souls brought collected.

The crypt holds many, together in time,

Resting & roaming

The darkened night skies.

The Crypt is a heart,

A heart of memory,

For all these dreaming

But it holds no enemies.

The crypt is calm,

The crypt is quiet.

For all that rests here

Knew once of riot.

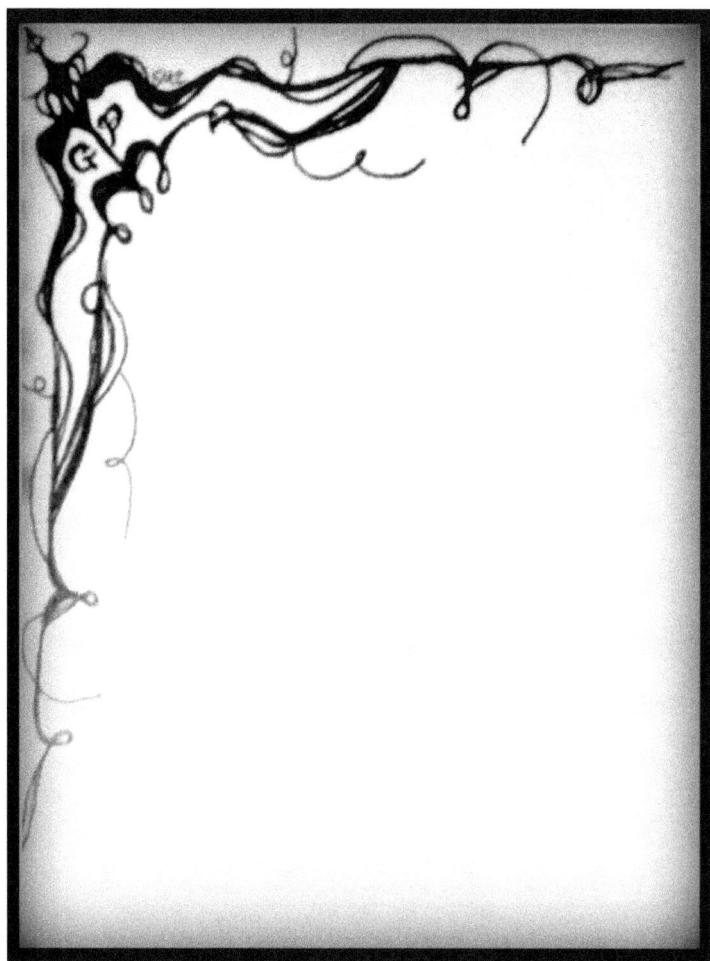

# The Pink Princess & the Darkened Foe.

Drenched in pink,

A painted doll,

Had a dream one night of a darkened foe.

Pink in her nature,

Pink in her dress,

Misshapen amongst the Gothic Princess.

This dream of such darkness

Brewed pink's curiosity,

Bringing pink to visit her neighbour's sanctuary.

Speaking of foes with black wings & nails,

Her neighbour replied "Sounds like you were taken by the sails"

'Sails? Pink asked, what are they?'

"Why they are the sails that sail you away …

… Away to a dark land of time …

You may visit their one night if you dream of foe & kind …"

Pink furrowed her brow, nodding her head.

"Ok next time I dream I will dream in dread,

To ask this foe what her problem is,

At least then I can get some proper sleep."

One night when dreaming in a nightmarish state,

Pink stood before the foe of late.

"Why do you show yourself to me?" Pink asked in kind.

"Well that's obvious, I must be on your mind." The foe replied.

Pink turned around & saw her past week's thoughts, no wonder her dreams had been so distraught.

"Ok Foe, I understand your side, but how may I ask as I to sleep in kind?"

Foe smiled & lowering her head.

"Well you must think of something pleasant instead"

Pink giggled & laughed with her,

How could she forget something so simple to learn?

Pink returned & slept well that night,

You see all you must do is think nice thoughts to avoid fright.

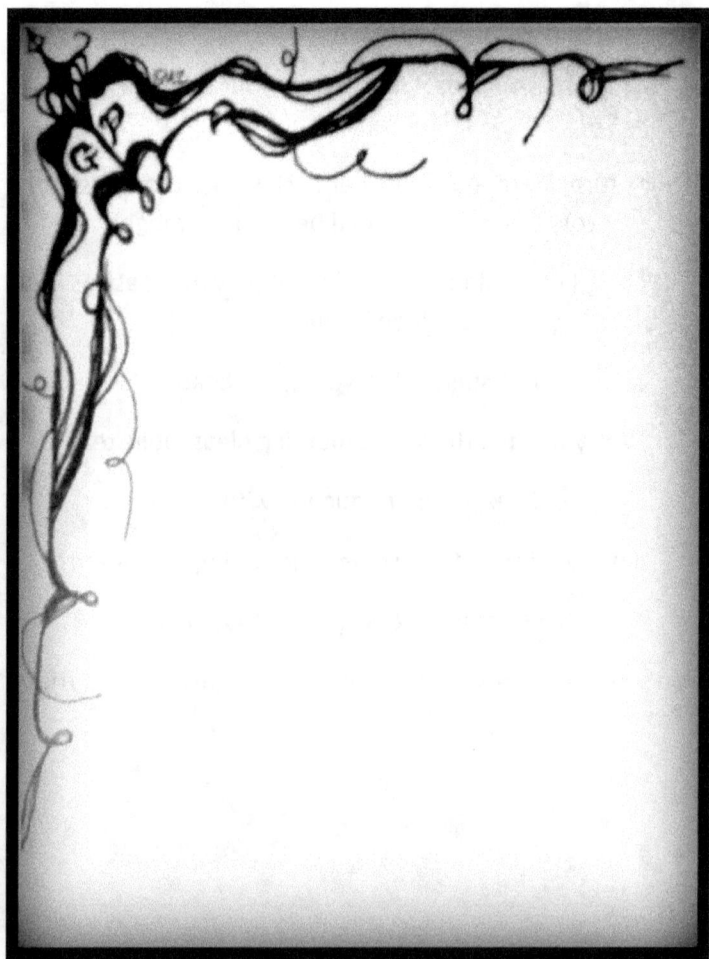

# Black & Red gown.

This black & red gown

Never a tear, never a frown,

My gown & I,

My gown & I.

Charcoal black tones, never creases it's my own.

Deep Blood red, the hues of dread,

Me & my dress,

Me & my dress.

Gown's at night,

Glows so bright, fits & falls so well.

Glisten upright, glowing in the moonlight,

My black & red gown will never sell.

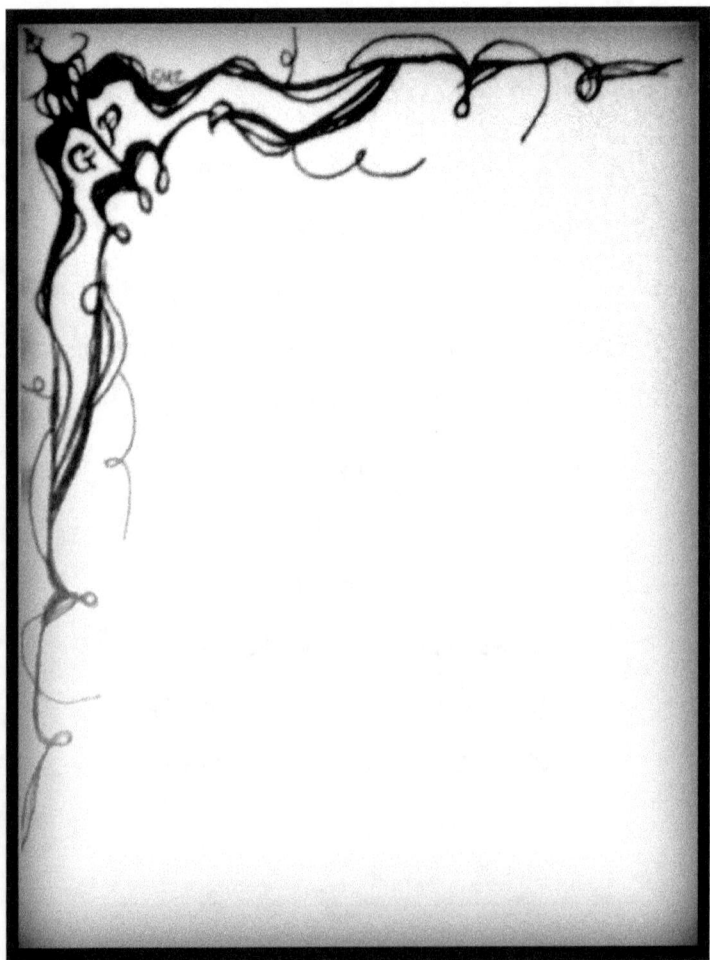

# Silver Tie of the Fox & the Ox.

The Fox, said Ox,

Tied his own brass locks, in a plait upon the grass in the green.

The Ox did skip, along a merry trip,

Though he envied Foxes hind legs so supreme.

The Silver tie said I,

Foxes nose arose, catching a scent of Ox nearby.

My Silver Tie can fly, said Fox to the Ox,

Grinning as his feet let the ground.

The Ox got cross at the ground & the Fox,

Fulfilling to chase Fox around.

Oh that Tie said Ox, so unfair he stare,

Why must I miss out of such a silver magical thing?

Well my tie dear Ox, said Fox to dear Ox,

I won at the chase through the green.

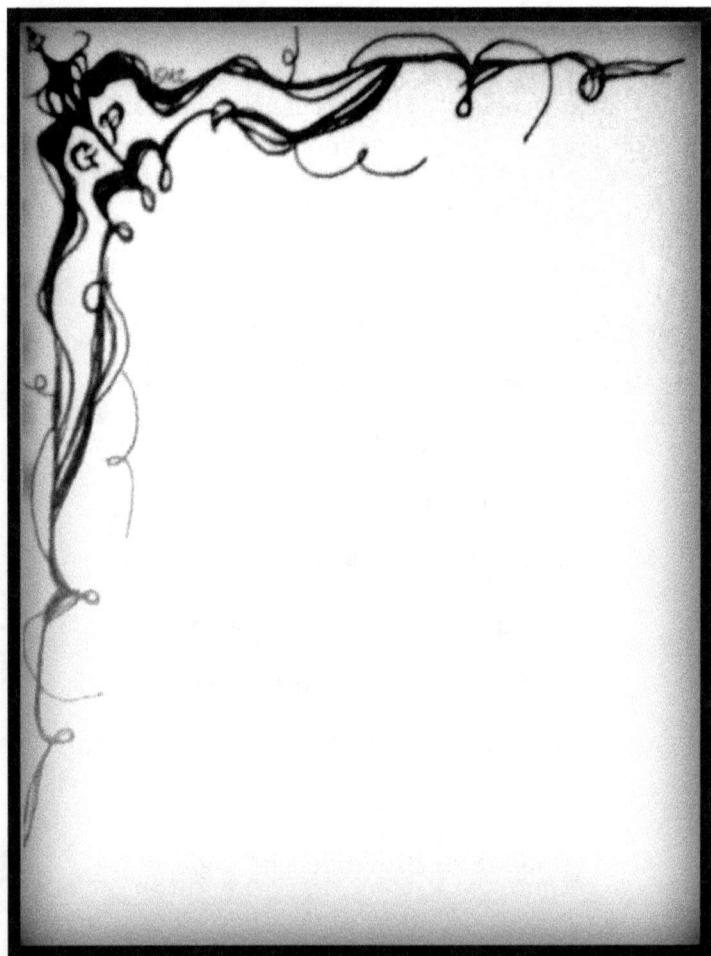

## Scattered Heart.

Scattered Heart,

Fell apart,

At my feet,

At the ground under my feet.

Heart a mess, I confess,

Fell apart,

My heart,

Fell apart.

Mama Corset Skeleton Illustration from my 'Steampunk Collection' ink on paper.

# Corset.

Corset,

Curves as it serves my waist with restraint.

Keeping a glorious shape.

Corset,

Pulls me in, keeps me slim,

Maintaining peoples stares as they gape.

Corset,

Slender, tender, maintaining my dream silhouette,

Beholding the beauty is my true duty,

My Corset & I are the best.

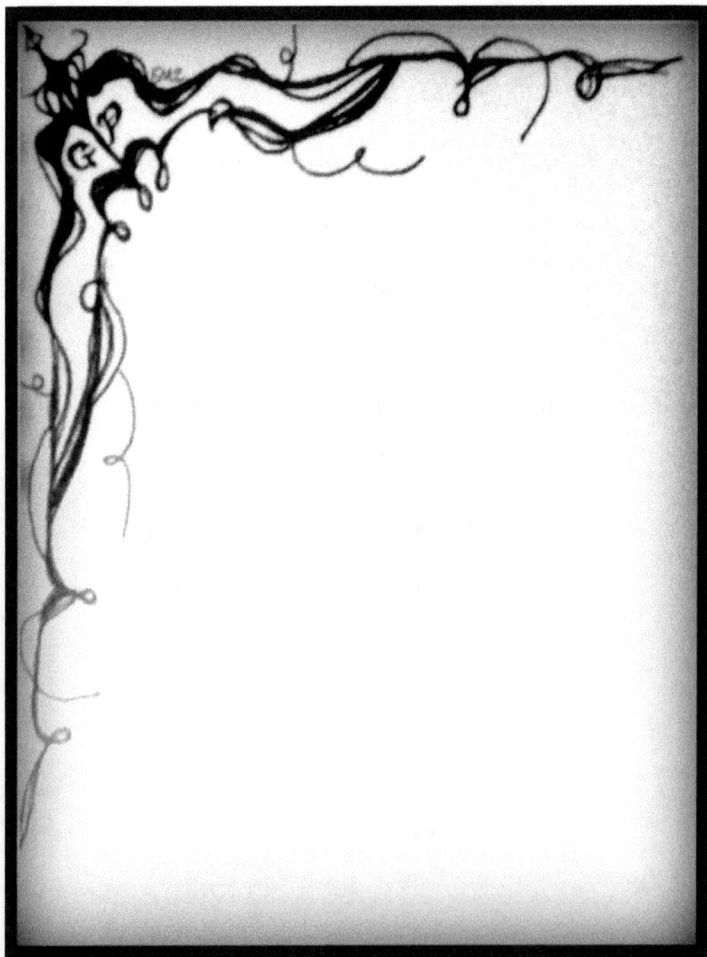

# Black Boots.

My Black Goth boots,

My true darkened roots,

Get me from A to B in style.

Adorned with buckles, chains & studs,

All around stare as I step with a thud,

Always me & my Boots.

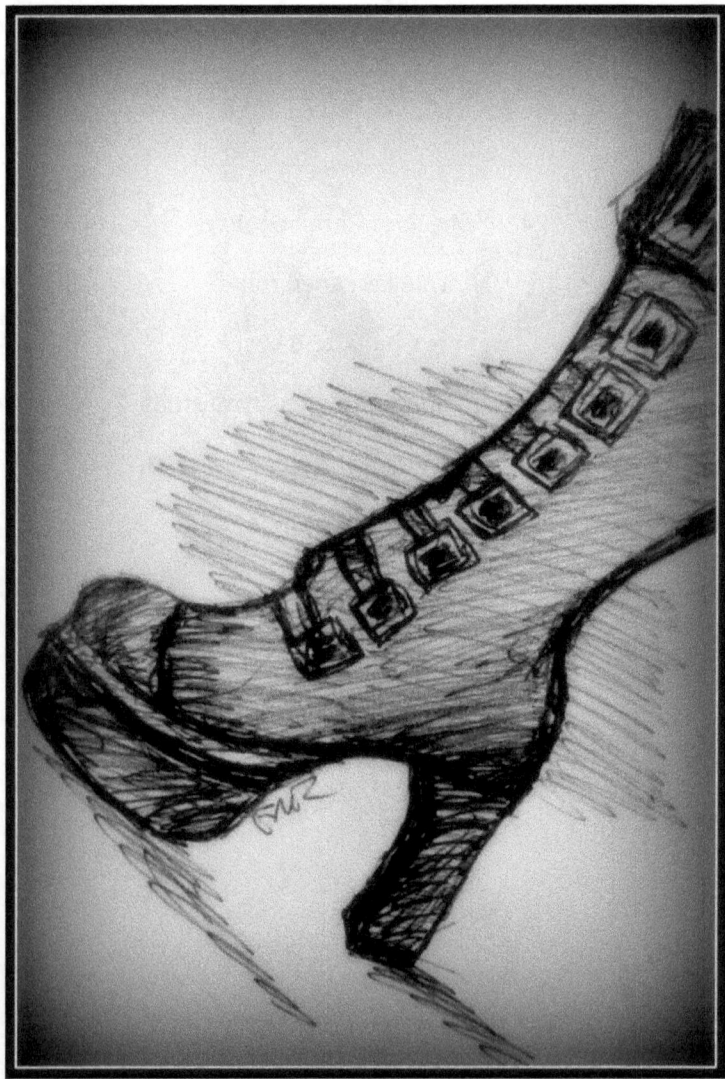

Black Boots Illustration, ink on paper

## Sleeping Maiden.

The Sleeping maiden,

The sleeping maiden.

For all silken scarves,

For the clothes,

She's laid in.

Sleeping soundly, so profoundly,

Dreaming quietly, blissful & silently.

Maiden sings,

Dreaming of wings,

Drifting past the blue sky,

Turning in covers,

Above all others,

Time slowly ticks by.

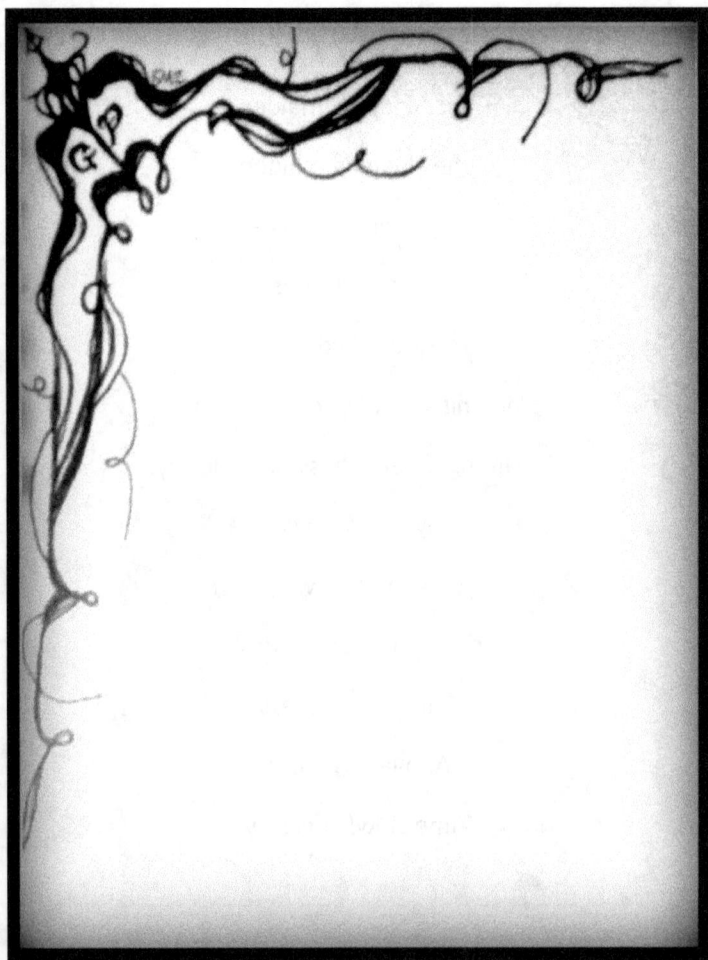

# Cryptic Script.

Lyrical masters,

Typing away,

Creating poems of lyrical play.

Written in emotion,

Anger & care,

Anguish in settlement,

All captured & laid bare.

Scriptures a plenty,

Histories in rhyme,

Written together,

For that one space in time.

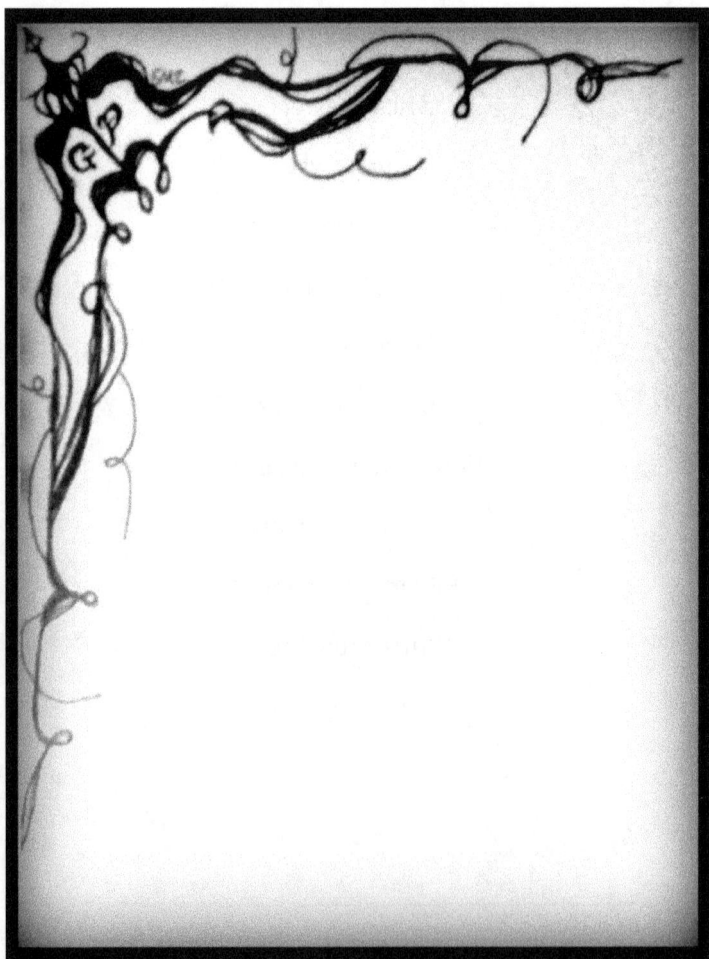

# Ghostly Hosts from the Cornish Coast.

Hosting the grand ball is all,

We have to host the ball,

More is all, the meek the tall,

All will come to the ball.

Your ghostly hosts comb the coast

As spirits float to the shore,

All aboard who not insured,

Come to the ball from the shore.

We must host the ghostly ball said Sid to Shirl,

This is our calling for the light.

Host this ball with all assured,

Curling the seas & the moors.

Photograph of myself, taken by Susan Morrissey

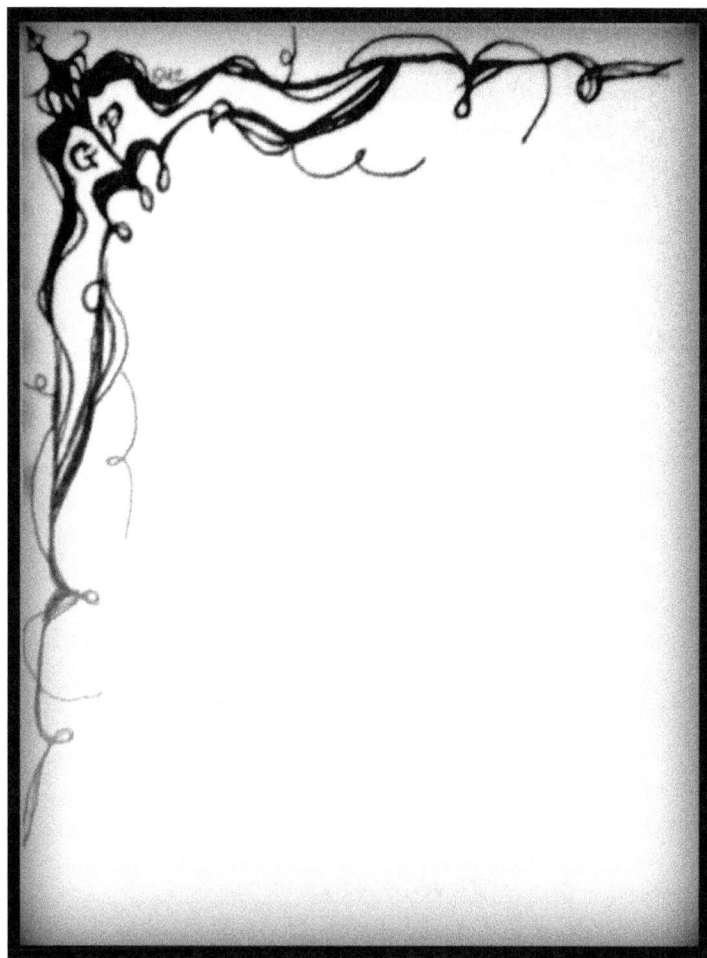

# Castle Grounds.

Mystic spheres,

Sculptured tombs,

Stones from souls,

Once doomed.

Historic grounds,

Tamed by them,

Droplets dusted

On the chandelier ends.

Old stones & marble flooring,

The curved stairway & the kitchen orbing.

Grand in vision,

Grand in place, the grounds of this castle,

Never leaving a trace.

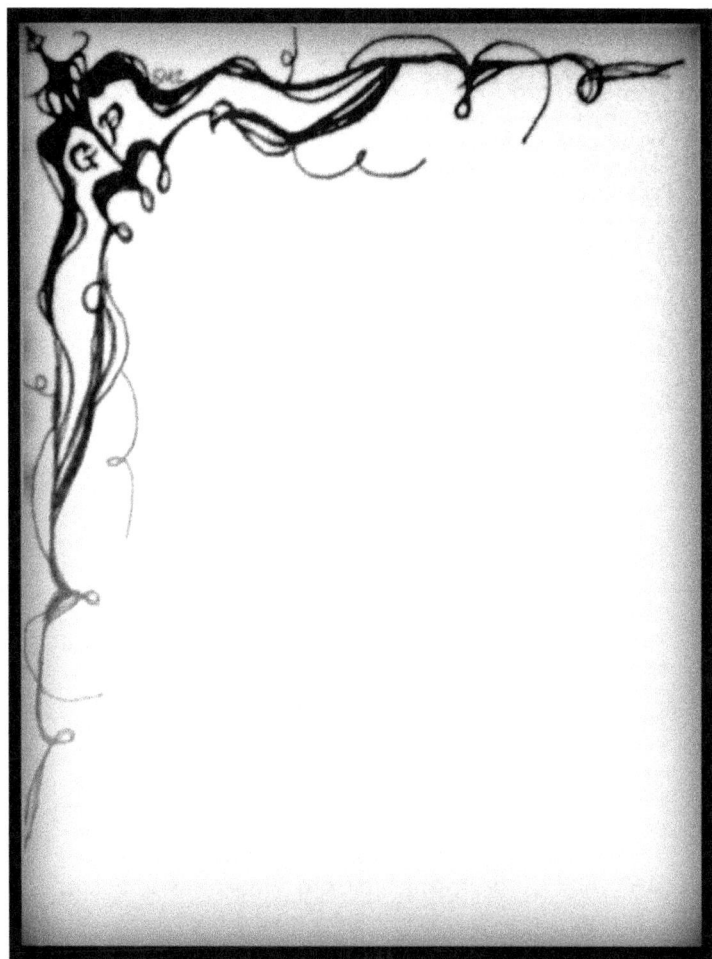

# Hammer.

My favourite past time,

For a true fan.

Black & white flickers

& a very tall man.

Cloaked in black,

Lined with red,

This man seeks his prey as they tilt their head.

Sharpened incisors as he bears his teeth,

Maiden's shocked still,

Can't move for disbelief.

A legend is told

Of a the vampire called Dracula,

And the best performance from a much missed actor.

My Portrait of Sir Christopher Lee, graphite on paper

# Ruby Choker.

My ruby choker,

Hugs my throat,

Catching the light

As it catches my coat.

Red as blood,

A stone of heart,

Nestled in metal,

As it enters the dark.

My ruby choker,

Sitting proudly above my collar bone,

Clutching my neck,

It's the only ruby I own.

Ruby Choker,

I wear with pride,

Gothic events out,

Or journeys far & wide,

My & my Ruby Choker,

Need never hide.

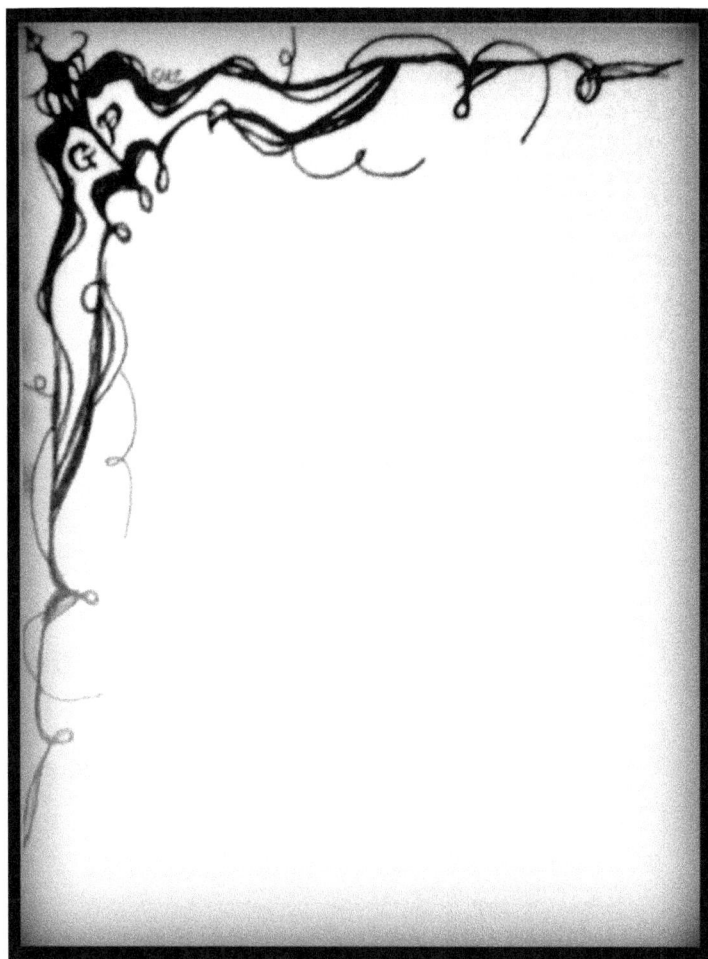

# *Lolita Glitters.*

Lolita fashion,

A unique & true fans passion,

Japan a place I admire,

A place I wish to go,

Lighting my desires like fire,

Dressed like a porcelain doll.

Frills, petti's, gloved delights,

What a truly beautiful sight.

Gothic,

Punk,

Sweet & many more,

So many wonderful variations to be discovered in store.

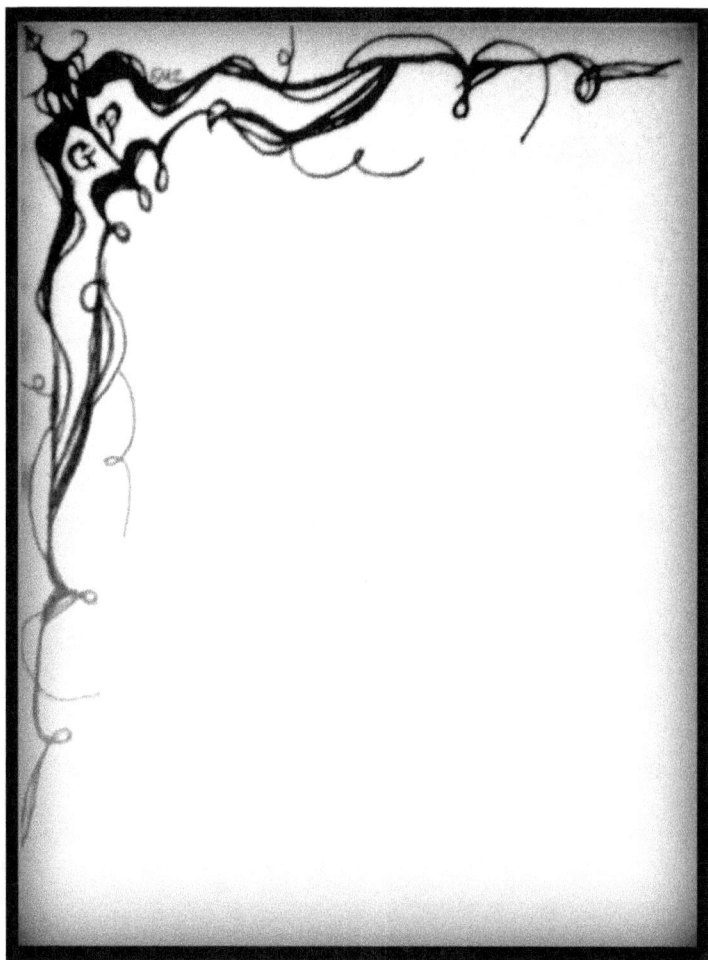

# Ghoulish Jewels.

Sparkling bright,

My black skulled rose,

Sitting on my neck buy not in repose.

Purple beauties bonded with bats,

Corset pendants & chandelier stacks.

Ruby jewels sat under my ear,

Near my juggler,

As Dracula draws near.

My little sparklers,

Jingle with each step,

My Ghoulish jewels,

Are always kept.

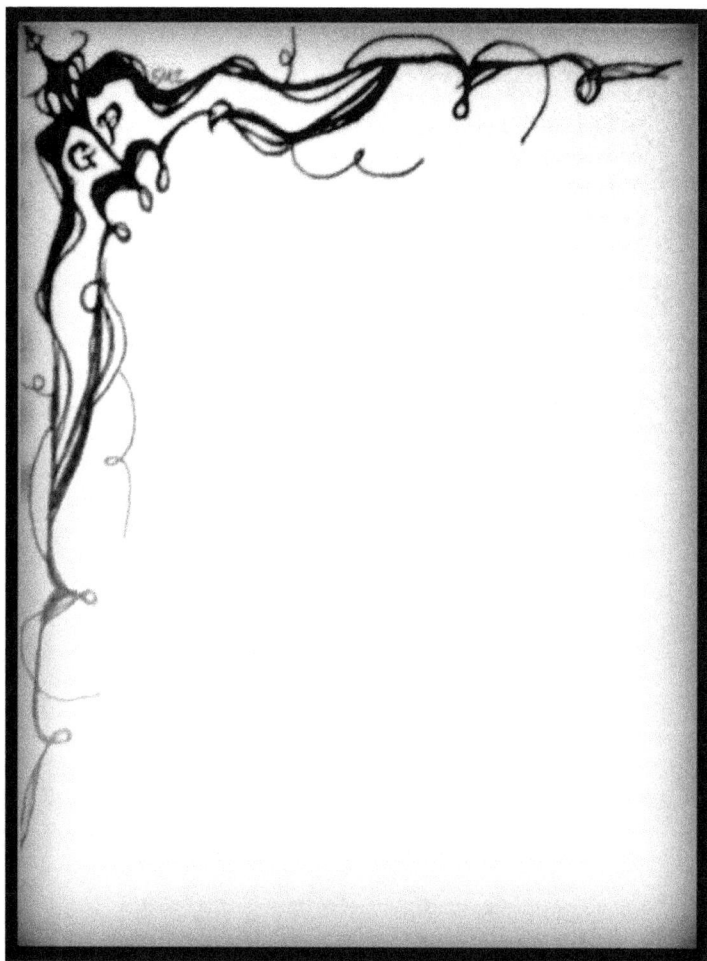

# The Bat's Hat.

Black Bat,

Sat at the tower,

Just hanging around.

When a mouse came up,

Sat up the top,

Said "I've never seen anything hang upside down"

"Why do you do that?" said the mouse to the bat,

Frowning & added

"Is that a hat?"

Bat smiled, slightly beguiled,

"Why yes dear mouse, it's just that"

"Holy Cow!" said mouse to the bat upside down.

"I've never seen a bat in a black top hat!"

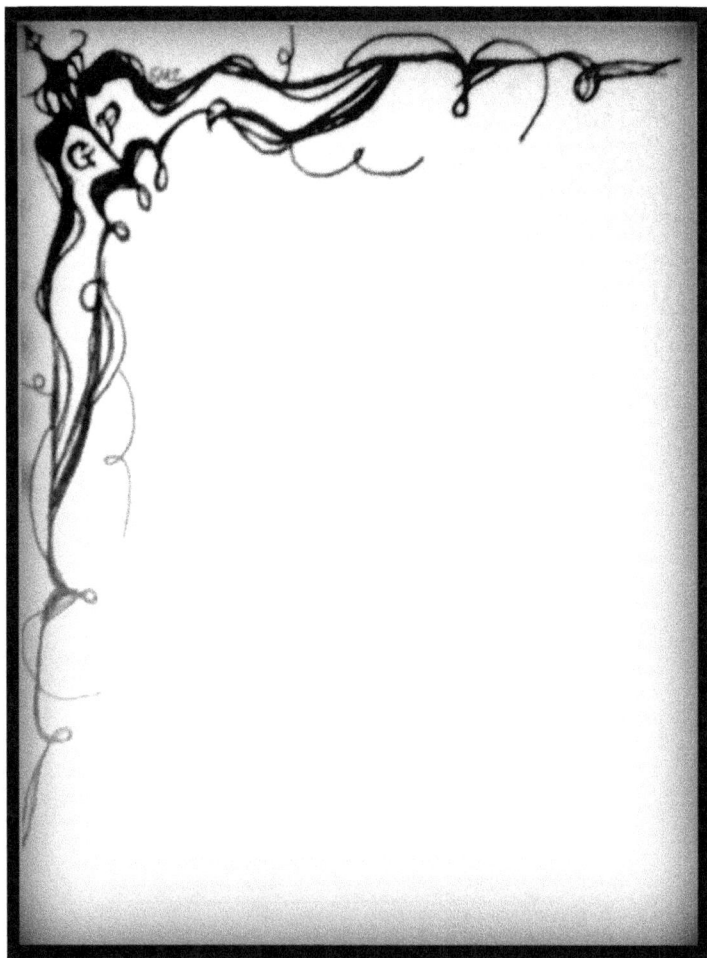

# The Laughing Skull.

Holes for eyes,

Was Skulls surprize,

His gnashes chattering as skull laughed out load.

A happy soul,

With not far to go,

Laughing aloud & proud.

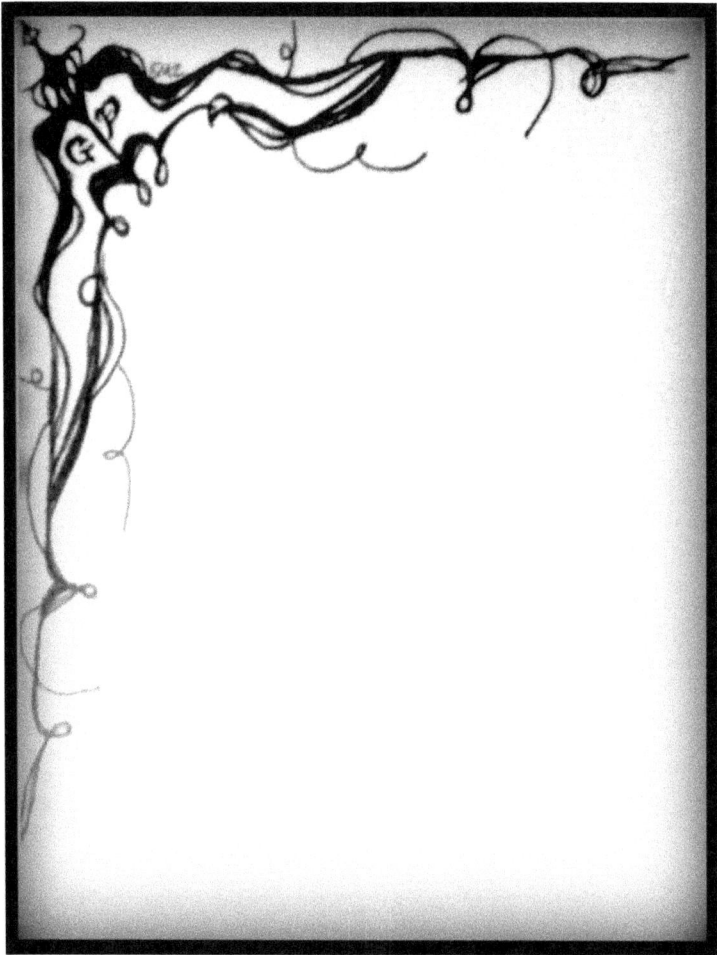

# Dragon's breath.

Breathing heavy,

Nostrils flaring & steady,

Chained to a wall in the cave.

Not able to fly,

Beg, borrow or buy.

To the stone walls

Dragon's slave.

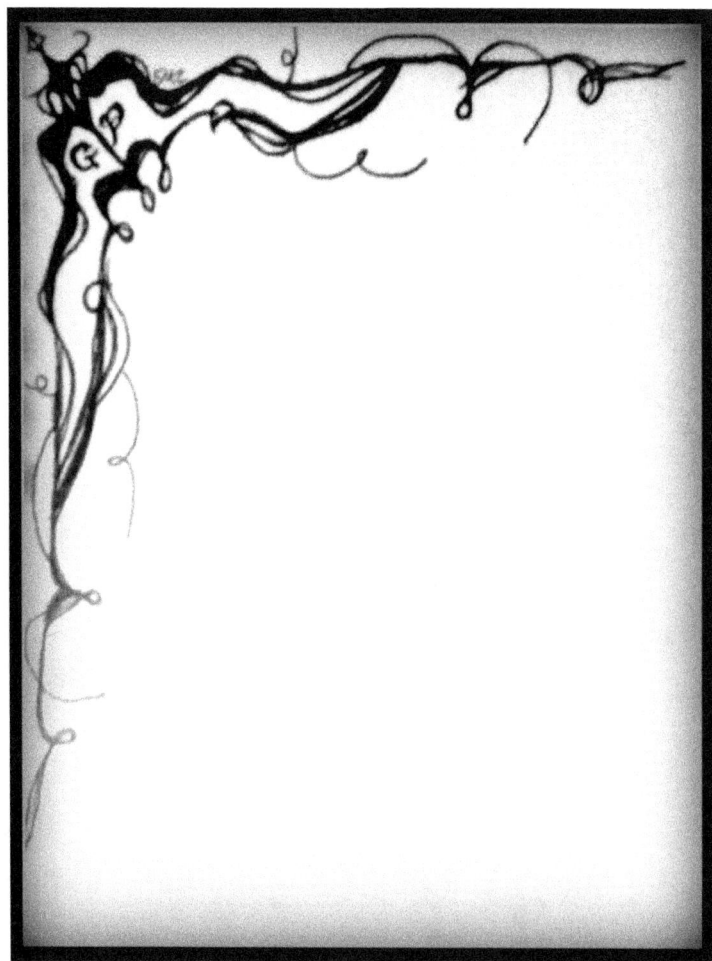

# Dancing Skeletons.

The dancing skeletons,

The dancing skeletons,

Jive at night,

To the flicker of lanterns.

Rattling bones,

Off from their thrones,

Dancing together in their tons.

The gang together,

Dancing forever,

The story of the dancing skeletons.

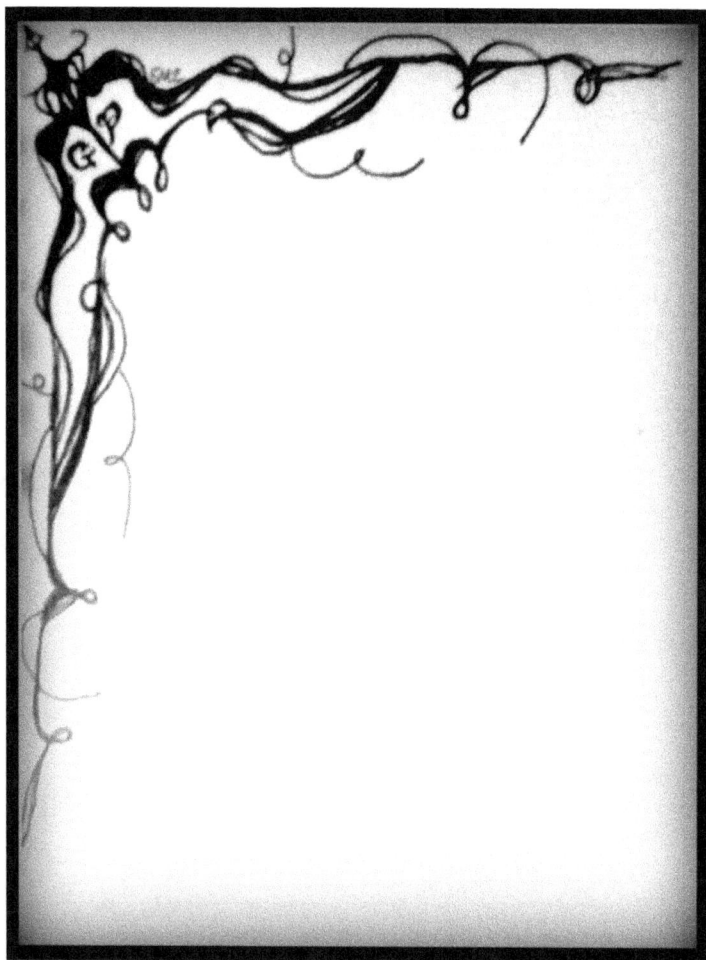

# Candelabra.

Flickering ambers,

Stood so proud,

Burning down the wax,

As it drips to the ground.

Brightly shining,

As hours go by,

Adorning the grand piano as people play it past nine.

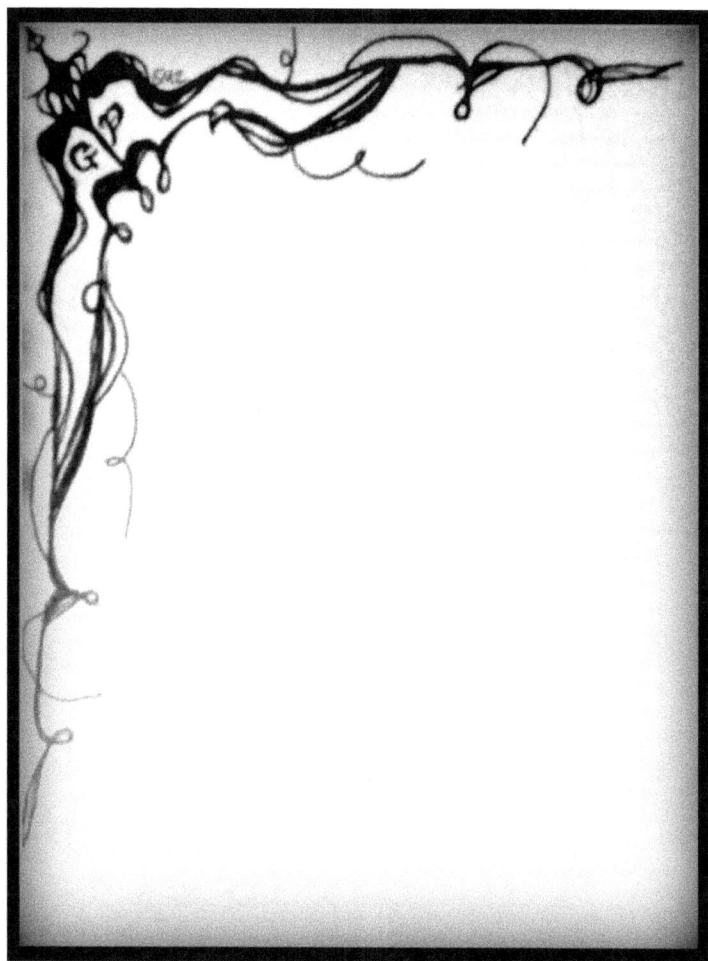

## The room that leads to nowhere.

Under the sky,

Under the dark,

Leaves an everlasting & dreadful mark.

It keeps all secrets,

Hidden within,

This room is threatened,

With the darkest of sins.

Filled with promise

To all dark souls,

Telling stories of nightmares yet to be told.

Go inside, do you dare?

Go to the room that leads to nowhere.

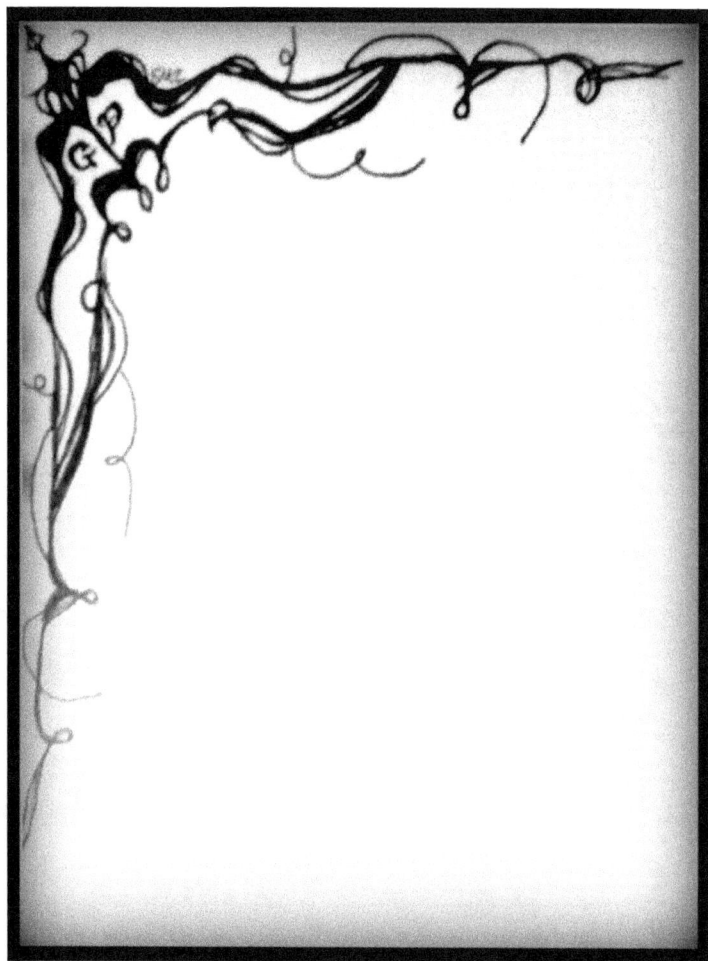

103

# *Dust.*

Dust,

It covers, it protects,

It slivers & collects,

Dusty floor,

Dusty surface,

Dusty mind.

Prone to sneezes,

Friends for creatures,

Hovers never ceases,

Dust,

Is ours all our lives.

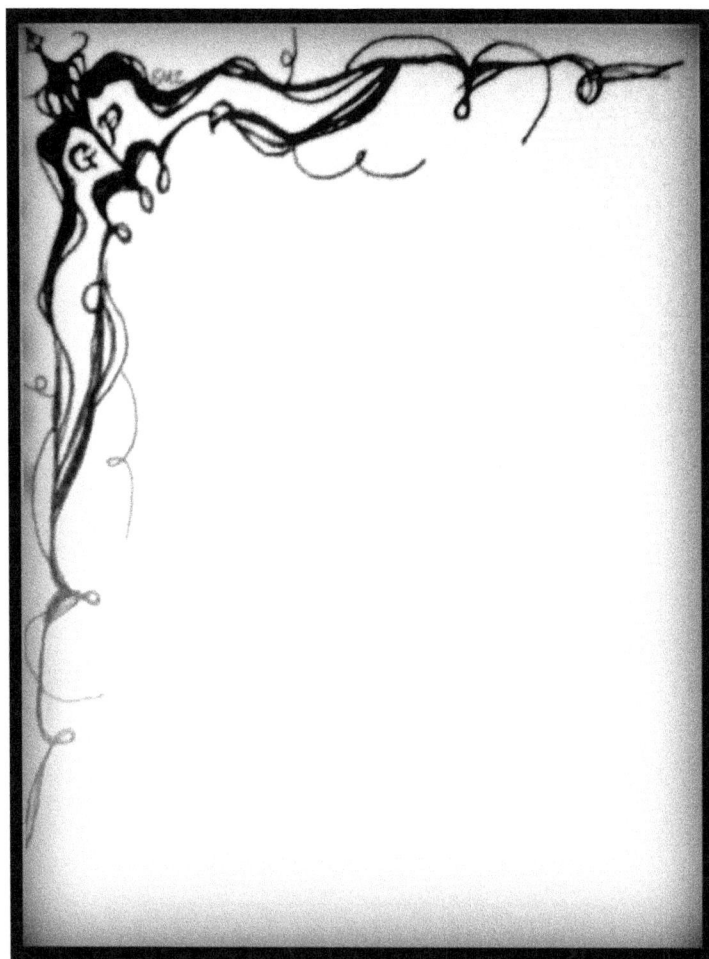

## Vultures.

A vulture culture

Is how we live?

Each draining each other,

To survive & not give.

The vultures leer,

They scheme through life.

Stabbing their friends in the back,

A theoretical knife.

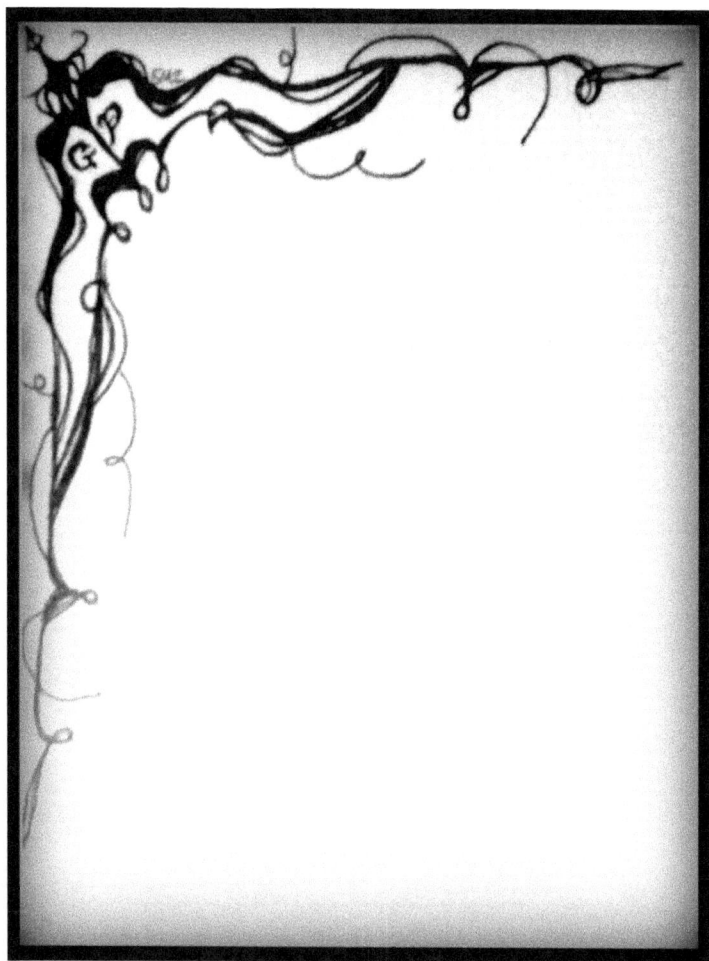

# Black Diamond.

They glisten,

Sparkle with a dark delight,

I swear they listen to me,

In my struggles & my plight.

Black diamonds,

Are my undoing

As they glow so bright,

Any piece of glory,

Keep me company at night.

Black Diamond Illustration, ink on paper

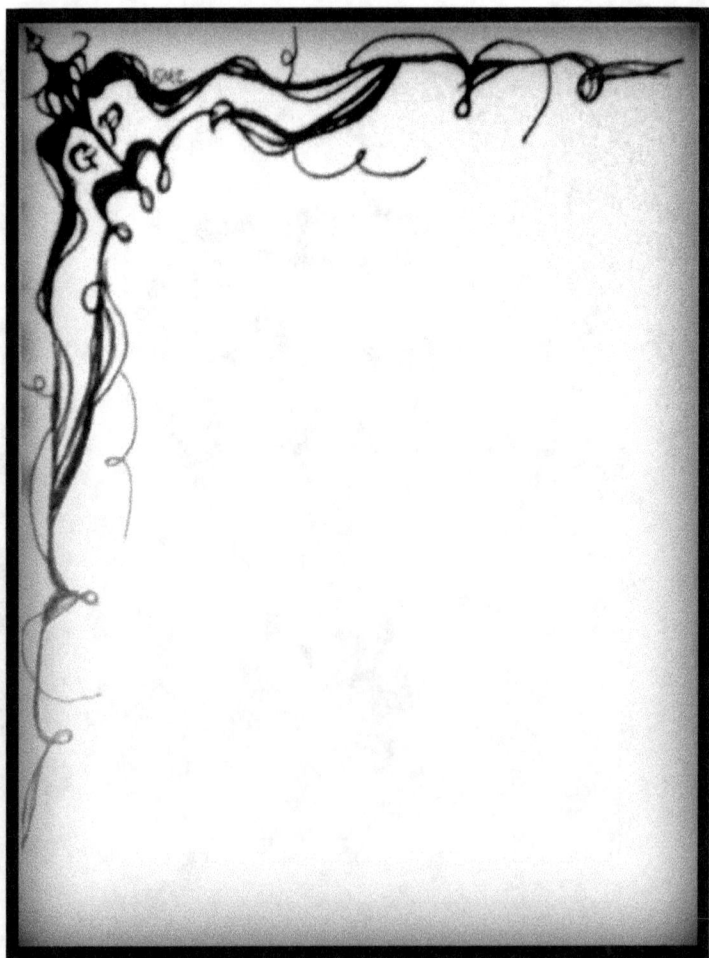

# Cloak & Dagger.

Cloak,

It hides,

It covers,

It hides.

Dagger,

It takes life,

It sneaks,

It takes life.

Together

They scheme

The power,

They scheme.

Together

They're mean,

Together

They're mean.

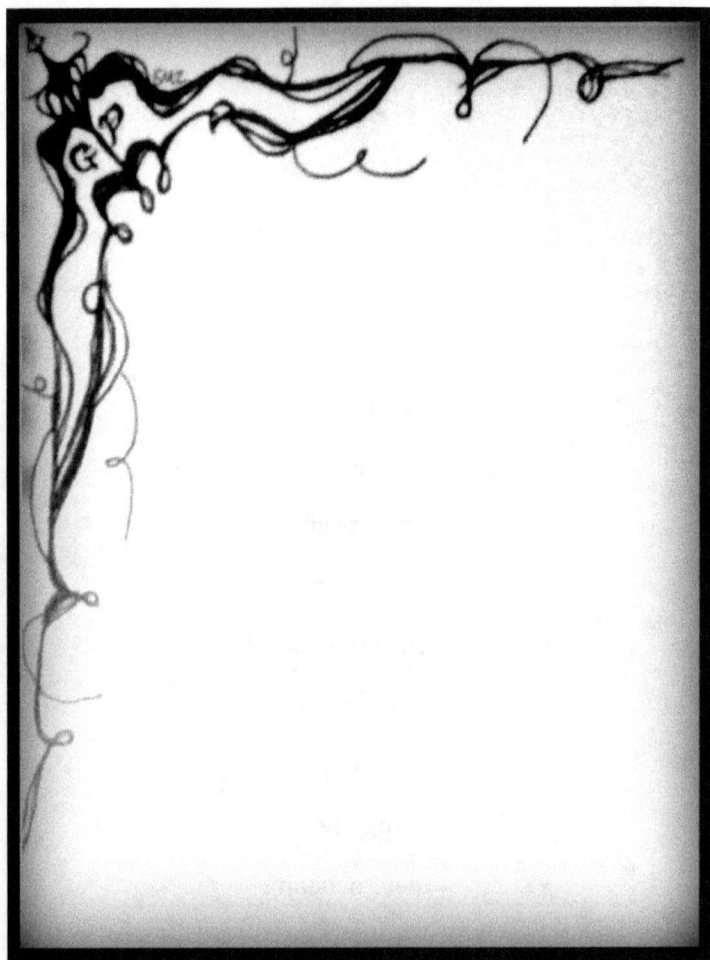

# *Night.*

A sheet of velvet,

Covers the sky,

Flickers of light,

Tiny shimmers up high.

Like a black cape hiding the sun,

Sweeping the light

Until a new days begun.

The Night of dark blue,

Black silky hues,

Covering the towns

The cities & pews.

Oh night,

How I miss you,

Comforting my plight

As you end a dark day in disuse.

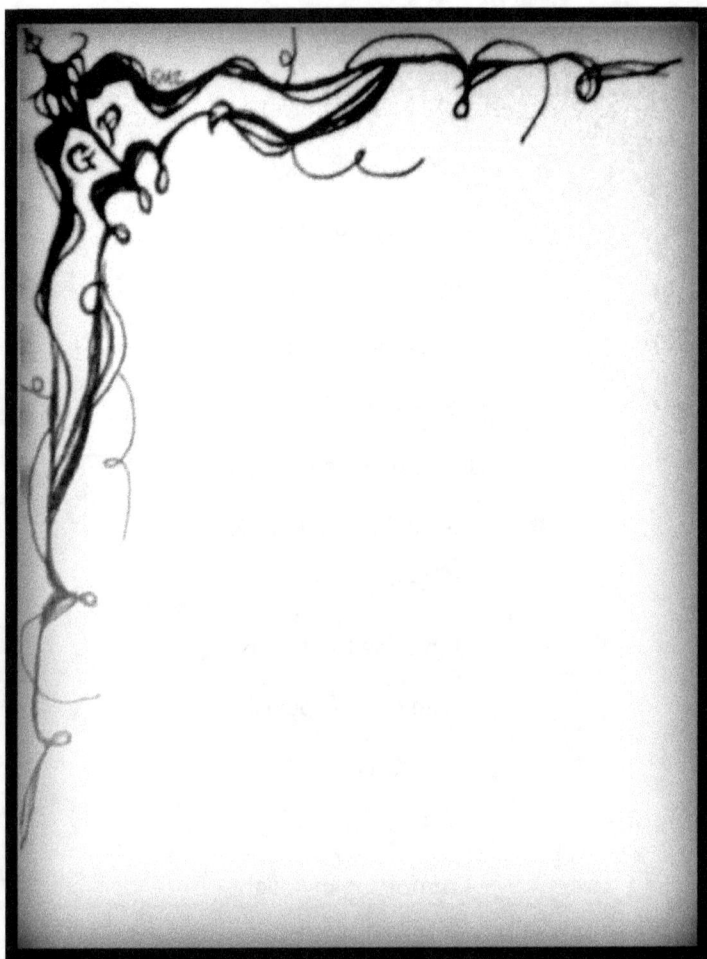

# *Vampire*

Vampire standing in the liar,

The fire flickering as the ambers grew near.

Teeth protruding & porcelain skin,

Bat transformations, awaiting maidens to draw in.

Red eyes,

Glowing with hunger & lust,

Senses your near, nightly feast is a must.

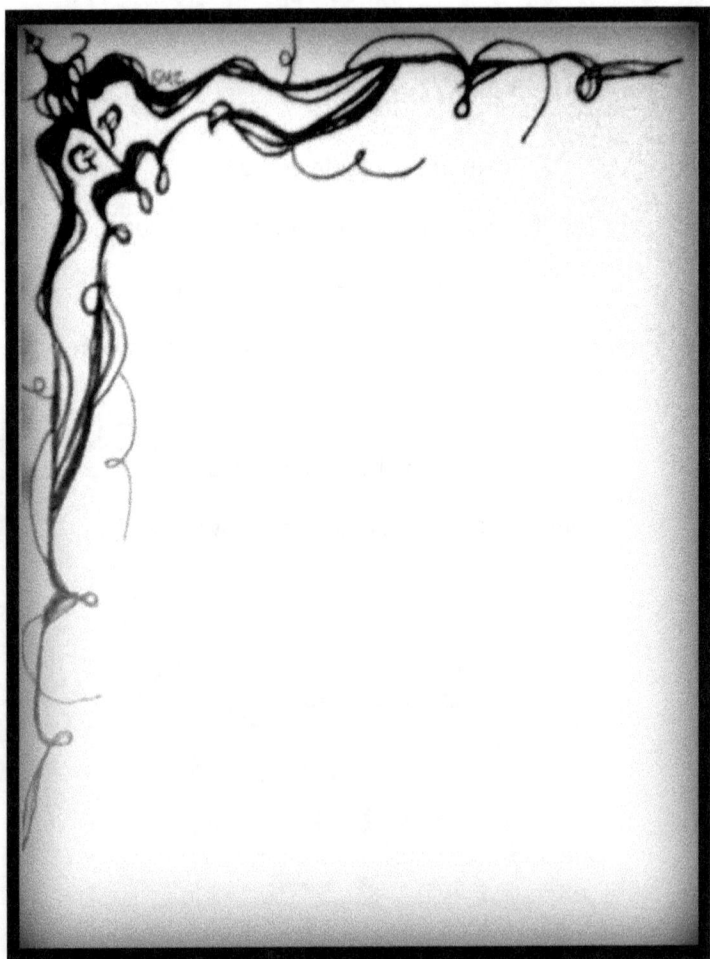

# Fairies

Fairies,

Glistening wings,

Rose head dresses & a matter of all pretty fairy things.

Curls in their hair,

As they dance around the tree trunks,

Collecting rose petals & pink flower buds.

Fairies enchanted by the winds sweet song,

Flowers floating in the wind so strong.

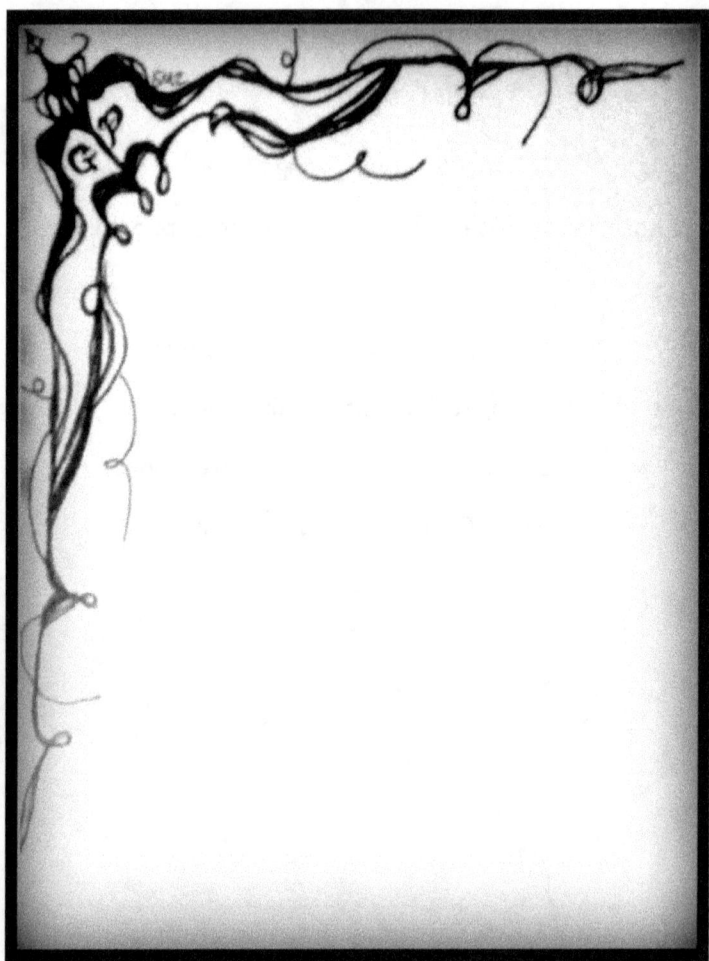

# Poison Punch

Poison Punch,

A deadly concoction,

From vampires crypt lays this evil potion.

Flowing black as it gives off a bloom,

Gathering mist for its drinkers to consume.

Poured in glass goblets,

Stored deep underground,

Vampires castle for drinkers gather round.

Drinking this poison,

Never making a sound.

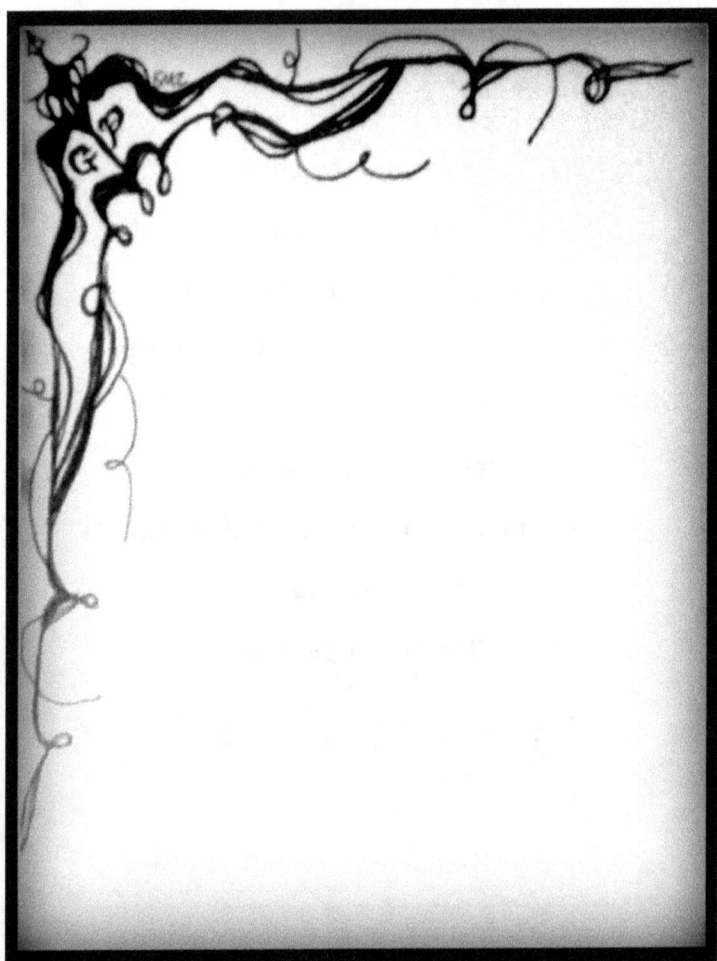

Rose painting in acrylic on canvas

# Vampire visit

Pain in my neck,

Pain in my chest,

Heaving back & forth,

What a quivering mess.

It's them you see,

They visit in my sleep,

Draining all that flows in my veins as they slowly creep.

My dreams are not nightmarish so don't be scared,

They settle my dreams,

So I won't stop them, as if I couldn't care.

Always the same place, as I nuzzle my love bite,

They'll be here soon & it'll start over for another night.

Pain as I wake, as I know what they've left,

My mind confused & a wound of some depth.

Vampires lurk here & I can't resist their call,

I really should get some garlic or some blessed water to be sure.

Perhaps then I will sleep soundly still,

Not awaiting a visit but to welcome my vampire to pass my windowsill,

It's an idea isn't it?

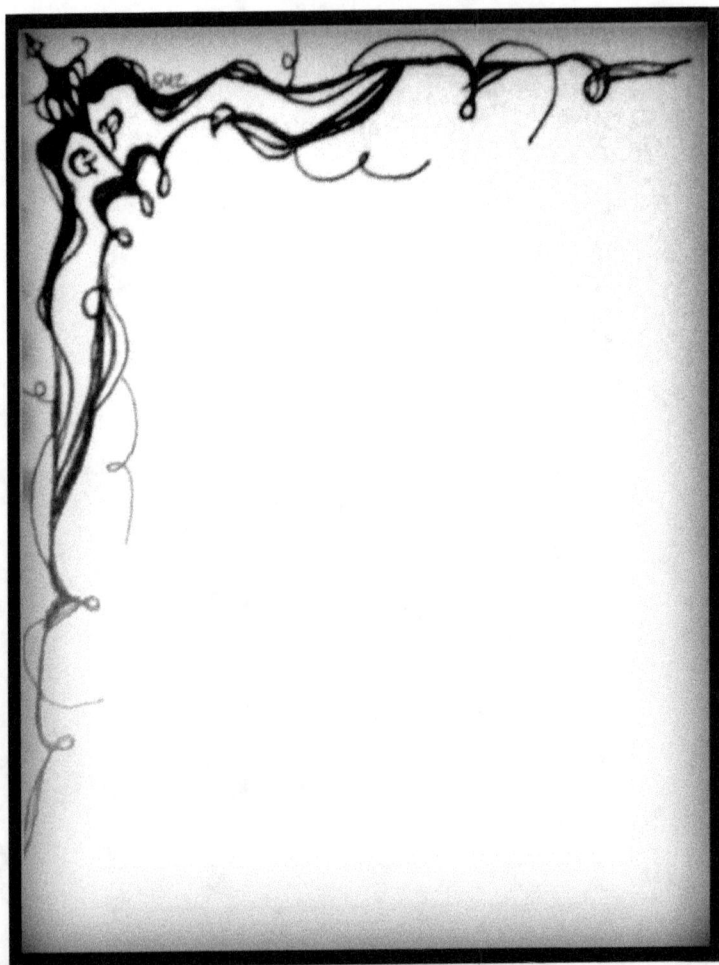

My portrait of Vincent Price, graphite on paper

# Witchy Sisters

The witchy sisters,

Stood in the kitchen chambers,

Plotting their next potion of love.

Each one powerful,

But not enough to get Mr Potts over still,

Their potion must not be strong enough.

They slaved away,

For 8 hours a day,

Practising their craft.

The cat watching near,

Eye of owl & mouse's right ear,

Would be enough for Mr Potts to take a draft.

Over he came,

As the potion floated up stream,

Landing upon the air he breathed.

He couldn't control it,

And wouldn't consume it,

As the witchy sister's came clean.

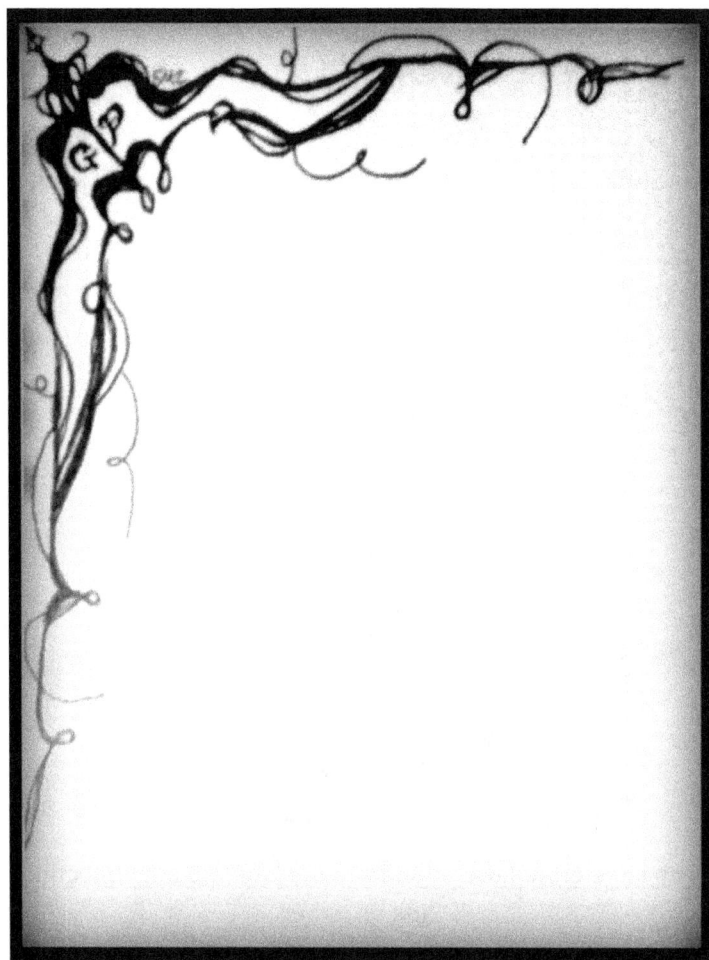

**Papa Skeleton Illustration from my 'Steampunk Collection'
ink on paper**

# Eyes

Staring,

Glaring,

As they search my nightmares.

Follow me around up & down the stairs.

Souls they see & evoke such emotion.

I can't resist this urge to behold them.

They scare me,

Glare at me,

And I cannot hide.

The red eyes of vampires,

Stealing all pride.

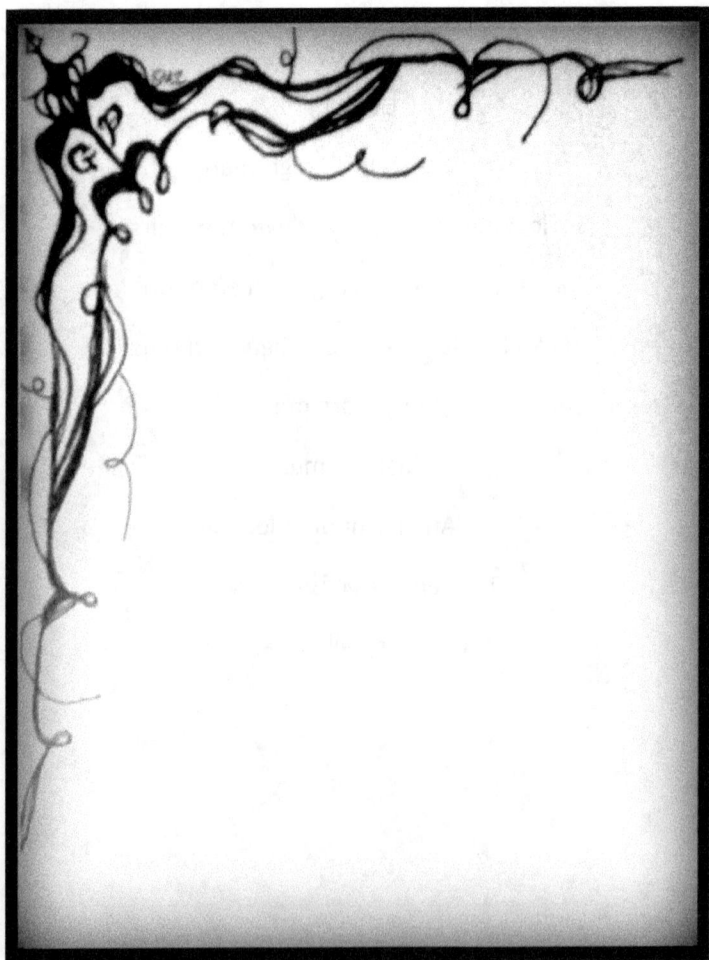

# Ghostly Mist

Ghostly mist,

Drifting over mountains,

The first on a ghost's lengthy list.

Floating above,

Blowing beneath,

Encapsulating every morsel from the sword to the sheath.

A mist of souls,

A gust of wind,

Enveloping all it carries within.

This ghostly mist travels far & wide,

Over cliff tops & battling the tide.

The mist of ghosts floating in the sky,

Towards the light as others pass them by.

Following the mist as it guides them towards,

Ghosts now travelling with a cause.

My portrait from 'Interview with the vampire' graphite on paper

# Drawn

Cloaked in sadness as the vamps draw in,

Breathing in pain feeling a vital sting.

Total drain & immobile in mind,

No strength as they zap all power inside.

Full control total surround,

Don't succumb to them,

Don't bow down.

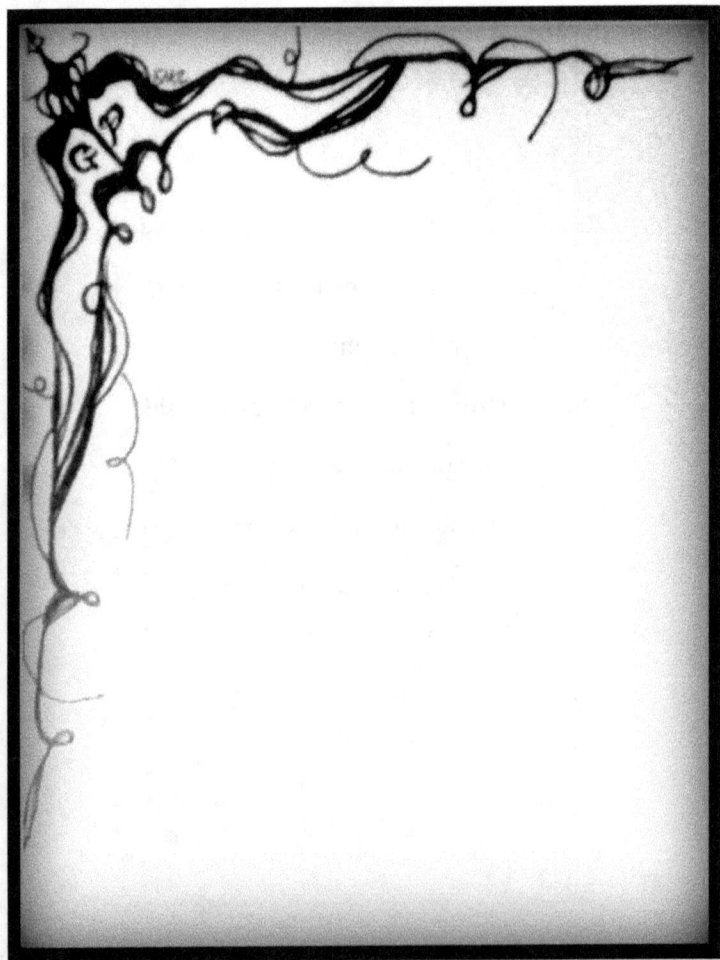

# Tudor Southampton

The Tudors have been here,

The walls echo their names.

Battles of will & stories of history untamed.

Ships sailed with royal crests of pride.

An infamous ship that echoes here for all,

Well-kept buildings with original foundations & walls.

Echoes of worlds past as we welcome new arrivals,

My love of old Southampton in all its glamour & coils.

Dungeons below & monuments still standing through past battles.

Kings past through here leaving their legacy,

Casting shadows.

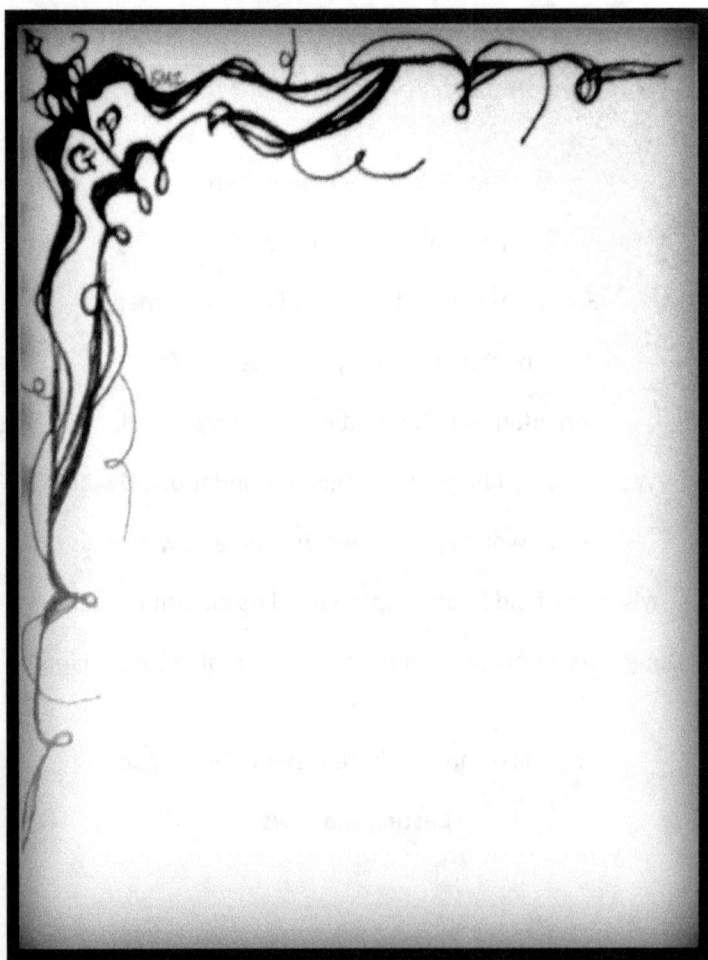

# Gothic cities

The old buildings that stand tall & proud,

Charcoal & chalk as the ships line the wet ground.

The cruise city with the old part of town,

Buildings that creek with character knowing no bounds.

History & heritage from a half century city,

My home cased in gothic glory & mystery.

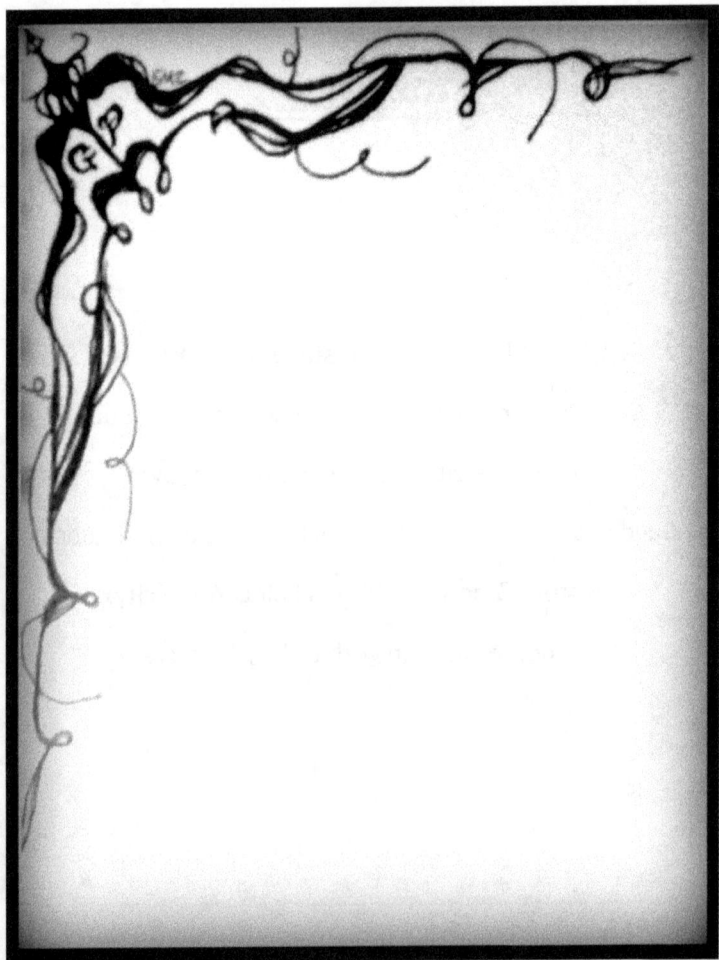

# *Brooding*

Perfect poetry of the dark brooding kind,

Inspired generations of the darker side.

Adorning shoulders of a melancholic voice.

Tales of dark feathers as we watch with one voice.

Gothic beauty & crimson drops,

Black lace & many corseted props.

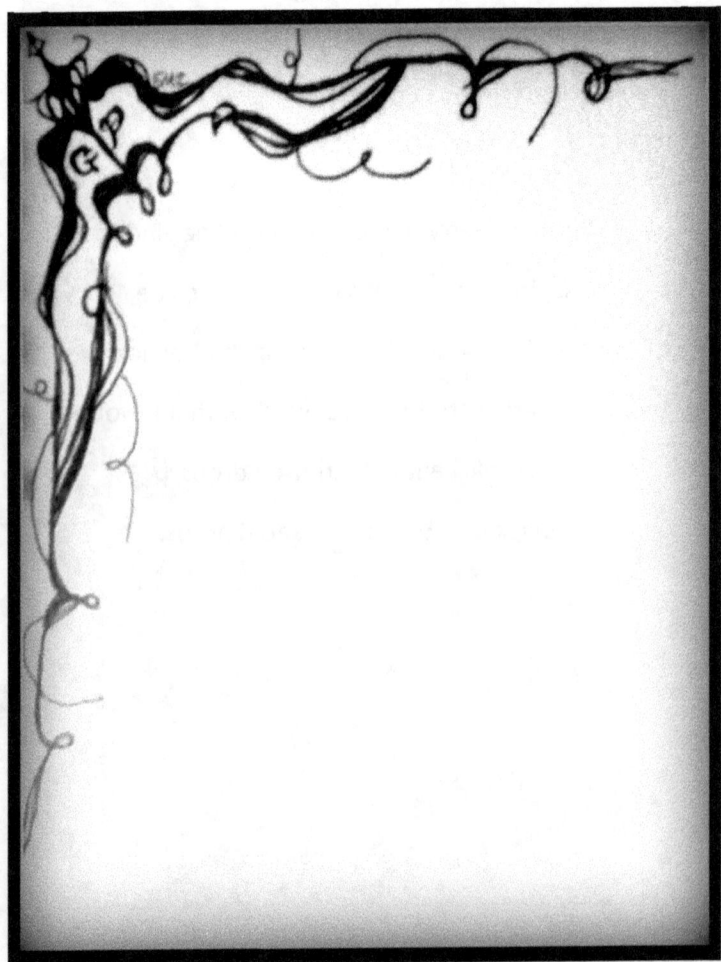

# Price to pay

Price to pay,

A voice of dark eerie draw,

Legends of horror & old creaky floorboards.

Many faces but the voice remained,

Famed characters & songs of horror fates.

Bird illustration, ink on paper

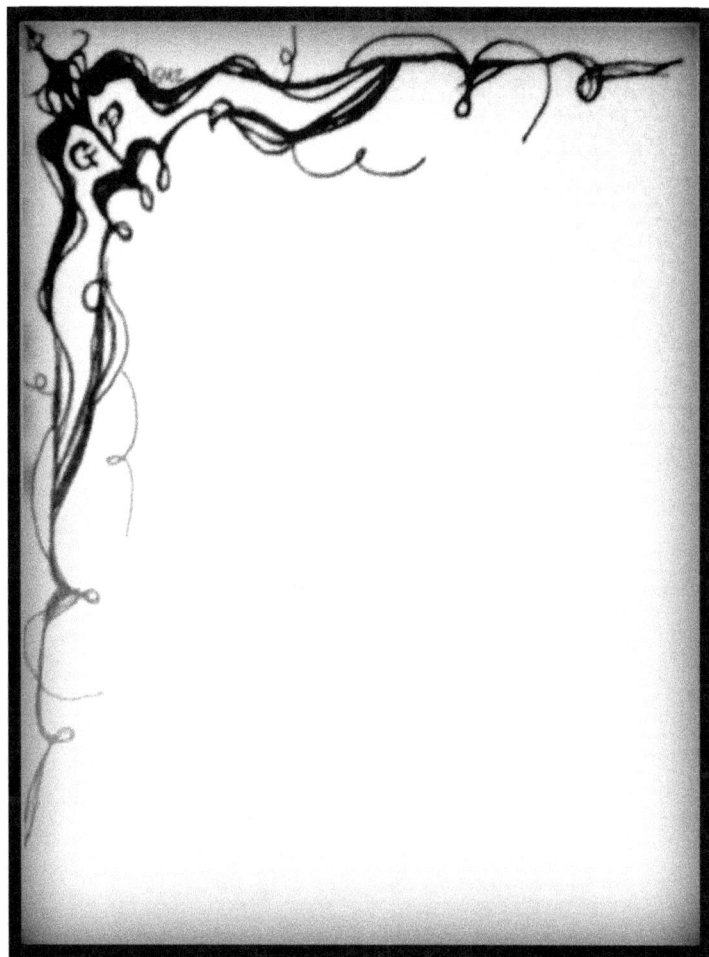

# Ode to the Dark princes

Ode to the dark princes,

A voice of deep & dark delight,

A towering statue over us in height,

Cloaked in horror & wonder to us all,

A power of darkness in each bite & claw.

Dark prince in nightmares

& evil in nature.

Standing in awe of this tall dark creature.

Never again shall we witness such mystery,

Other creatures remain,

But stand driven away by memory.

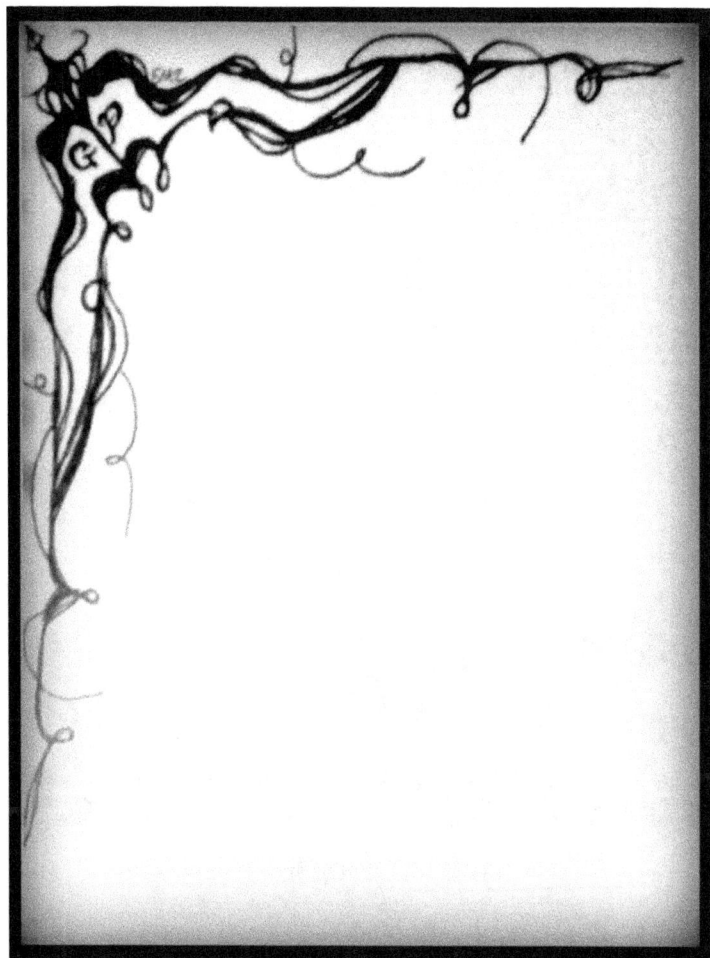

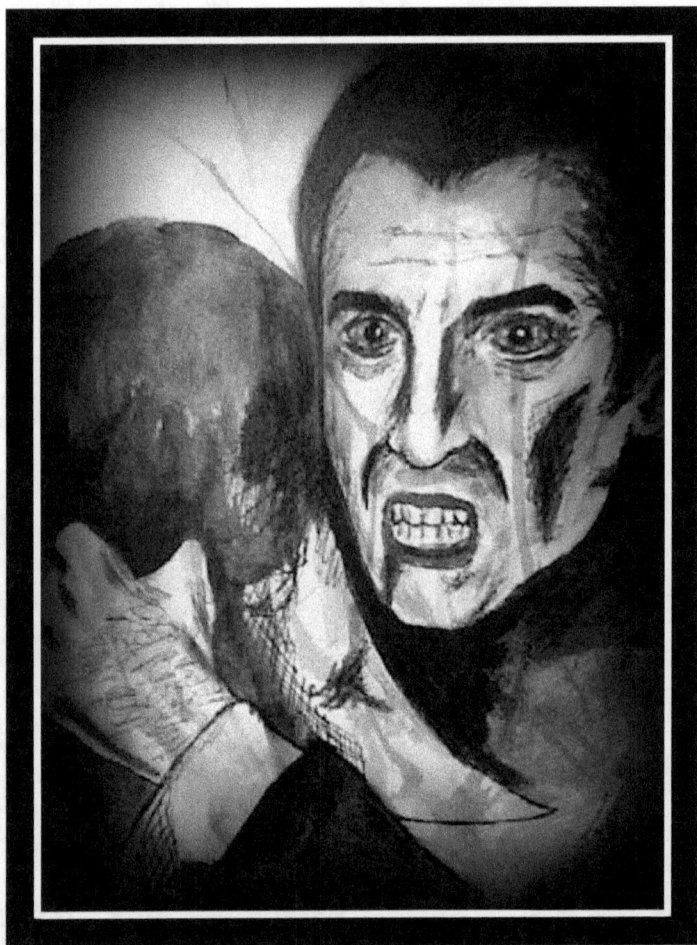

Dracula Illustration, ink & watercolour on board.

## Birds of prey

Birds of prey,

What do they think?

What do they say?

Do you think they speak with each chirp & song?

Maybe they call upon each other,

When they been over for so long.

This bird is unique,

It sits alone,

Bearing its head,

Nestling its feathers,

Does it have a home?

Wings of jet black,

With a long, strong beak,

Picking at the well soaked soil,

Searching for a treat.

Black bird searches,

Finds its meal,

Retreating back to the nearby tree,

As it perches & recoils.

Others leave it,

They fly straight past,

Do they know he's there?

Or are they giving him space?

Leaving their prints as a cast.

He sits alone,

Pecking at his food,

Seemingly untroubled,

But what would I know?

I don't want to intrude.

Black bird seems rested,

Maybe he's tired,

He does move slower,

But I wouldn't want to guess it.

Humble black bird,

Do you stay in at night?

Amongst your nocturnal friends,

Or do they give you a fright?

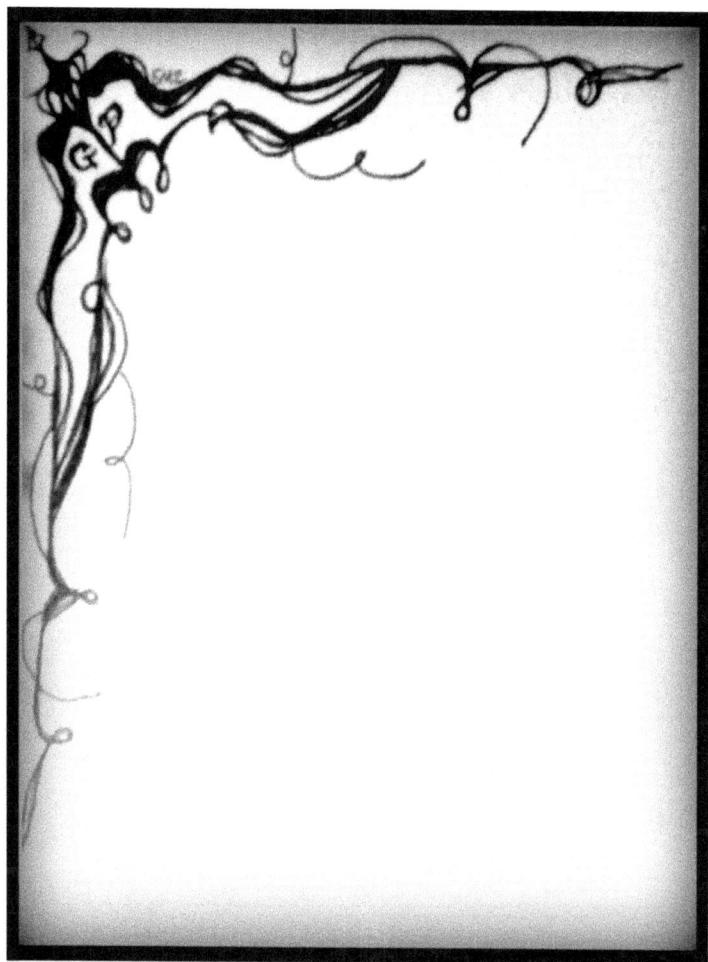

# Storms

Storms a throw ahead over cliff edge,

As waves crash & collect on the hefty ledge.

Angry sky overhead in the night,

Causing thunder to lash & fight.

Together create a wonder of sounds,

Radiating from the sky to the deepest ground.

Storms inside as the trees hold on,

Branches fleeing fearful to land upon.

Stormy skies as the night draws a close,

All together in brilliant repose.

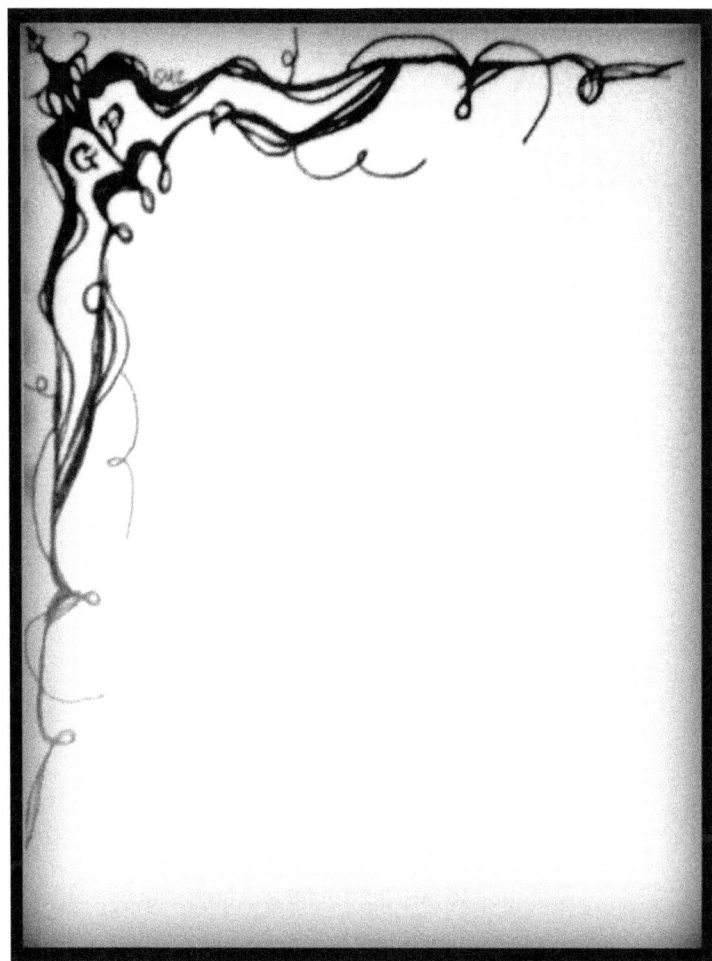

# Pebbles

A pebble thrown as it lands on the ground, cold & alone.

'What is the life of a pebble?

To live underfoot & kiss the ground,

To come & go with others,

Never naught but a scuffling sound.

'We are all of different sizes?'

Thought the pebble,

Admiring the others as they skid along the floor,

'Well they are all different ages'

'Some have always been here'

'And some are only four!'

'It's dark here now'

Said pebble, looking upon the castle grounds,

Well soon to be light from the nearing sun,

What an unusual thing for a pebble so profound.

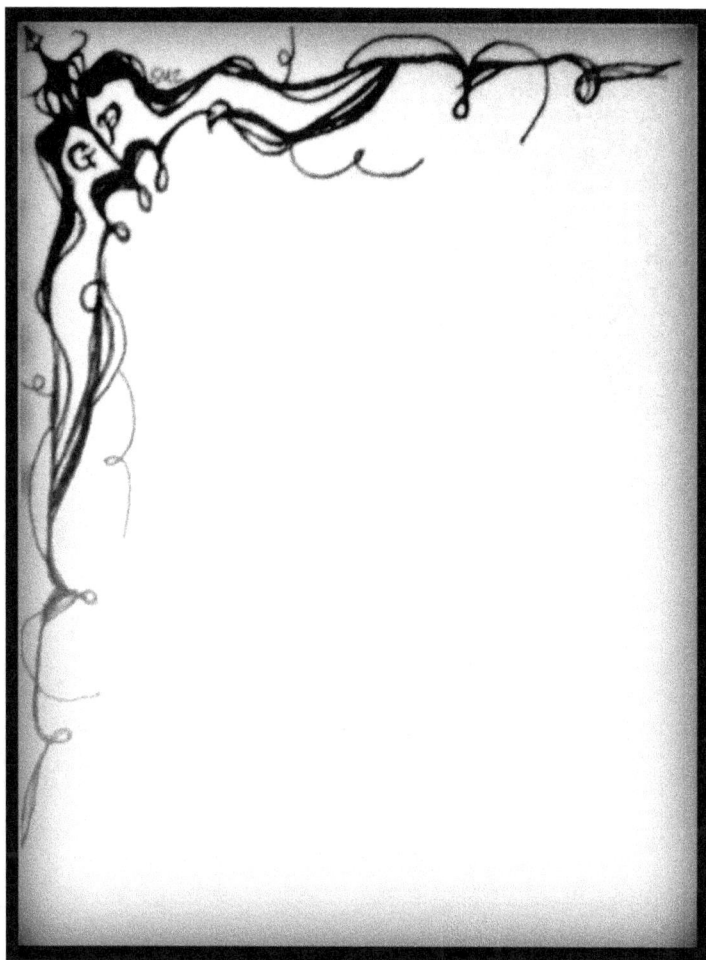

## About the Author

Emma Morrissey is a Fine Artist & business woman in the South of England, creating custom Art pieces, & teaching Art & Enterprise. Emma pursued her dreams & set up her business in 2014. Now a published book cover Artist, exhibiting across Hampshire & teaching/mentoring students in University, Emma is passionate about sharing her work with the world.

*"I have always loved fashion & Gothic culture, the films, the music, the poetry, the Artwork & the literature; so pursuing a passion of mine to put my poems & illustrations together in this book was very inspiring." Emma Morrissey 2015.*